A Good Read 1

Pre-Intermediate

SHOHAKUSHA

はじめに

　本書 A Good Read: Developing Strategies for Effective Reading - Book 1【Japan Edition】は同名の英語版に基づいた読み物（各章 300 語程度）を基盤としたリーディング教材です。TOEIC®TEST (Listening & Reading) 350-450 点レベルの学習者を対象としており、A Good Read: Developing Strategies for Effective Reading - Book 2、Book 3 とシリーズを構成しています。

　本書は様々な読解ストラテジー（＝ リーディングのコツ）が習得できるよう構成されています。読み物の内容は身近な話題が多く、中には思いがけないオチで終わるものもあり、楽しく読み進めることができます。また、学習の過程で単語だけでなくチャンク（＝ 2 ～ 8 単語で構成される決まり文句）も学ぶことができるように配慮されています。さらに、【Japan Edition】では、リーディング内容をスピーキングやライティングの活動につなげるタスクを各章に用意し、4 技能の統合や英語での表現や発信につなげる学習を可能にしているのも大きな特徴です。

　本書は 12 の Unit と 4 つの Review による計 16 の章で構成されています。各 Unit の Warm Up、Reading Strategy、Strategy in Focus は予習で使うことを想定しています。まず、Warm Up で Unit のトピックに関するスキーマ（＝ 背景知識）を活性化します。次に、Reading Strategy でその Unit で習得すべき読解ストラテジーを学び、その後、Strategy in Focus でそのストラテジーを使った活動に取り組んでください。続く Reading のセクションでは、予習で学んだ読解ストラテジーを確認しながら、パッセージを読み進めていきます。読解の後は、パッセージに出てきた重要な単語やチャンクを Word Work で確認します。さらに、本書では読解にとどまらず、スピーキングとライティング、個人活動とペアワークをバランスよく配置したアウトプット活動を用意しています。これらの活動を通して、英語で発信するスキルの習得を目指してください。

　Review では、直前の 3 つの Unit で学んだ読解ストラテジーを振り返り、その後、それらを総合的に用いながら新たなパッセージを読み進めます。More Word Chunks では、既出チャンクの復習に加えて、発展的に新たなチャンクも紹介されます。Review にもアウトプット活動が用意されています。

　本書での学習を通して、学習者のみなさんが英語で物語を読む楽しさを味わいながら読解ストラテジーを身につけるとともに、アウトプットのスキルも向上されることを祈っています。最後になりましたが、松柏社編集部のみなさんに心よりお礼を申し上げます。

2016 年秋

竹内　理
佐々木顕彦

A Good Read 1

Vocabulary

The following are the common expressions used in the activity directions.

❶ Match the words to Japanese definitions.

- a. **adjective**
- b. **author**
- c. **collocate**
- d. **describe**
- e. **identify**

- f. **refer to**
- g. **rewrite**
- h. **score**
- i. **verb**
- j. **word chunk**

- i. 特定する、明らかにする
- ii. 書きかえる
- iii. 採点する
- iv. 〜に言及する、〜のことを言っている
- v. 共起する、連語を成す
  (e.g.,「風呂に入る」というとき、a bath は take と共起する)
- vi. 形容詞
- vii. 動詞
- viii. 単語のかたまり（2-8 単語で構成される決まり文句）
- ix. 著者
- x. 説明する、描写する

❷ Complete the Japanese sentences using the words in the box below.

- **Circle** the **phrases** that are **mentioned** in the text.

    テキストで (a)_____られている (b)_____に (c)_____なさい。

- Look at the title of the **article** on the **opposite** page.

    (d)_____のページの (e)_____のタイトルを見なさい。

- **Decide** if these **statements** are true **(T)** or false **(F)**, **according to** the text.

    テキストに (f)_____、これらの (g)_____が (h)_____か (i)_____

    かを (j)_____なさい。

記事	○をつける	語句	決定する	したがって
正しい	述べる	反対側の	文章	間違っている

3

Contents

Unit	Theme		Strategy	Reading	Page
1	Personality		Making hypotheses (Guessing)	Your Music and Your Personality [256 words]	6
2	Happiness		Skimming	A Businessman's View [303 words]	12
3	Friendship		Scanning	What I Like Most About My Best Friend [278 words]	18
Review 1			Review of Reading Strategies 1–3 Jennifer Lopez [355 words]		24
4	Difficult Decisions		Making predictions	Choosing the Right Career [304 words]	28
5	Life-Changing Moments		Making inferences	Ana and Her Fiancé [315 words]	34
6	Unexpected Events		Interpreting	A Surprise Gold Medal [334 words]	40
Review 2			Review of Reading Strategies 4–6 Modern Social Networking [334 words]		46

Unit	Theme		Strategy	Reading	Page
7	Finding Love		Making judgments	A Nightclub Romance [331 words]	50
8	Kindness		Making associations	My Best Friend Dan [346 words]	56
9	Bravery		Deducing the meaning of words from context	A True Hero [381 words]	62
Review 3			Review of Reading Strategies 7–9 Riding the Wave [247 words]		68
10	Urban Legends		Visualizing	The Hairy Hitchhiker [343 words]	72
11	Relationship Myths		Summarizing	Dating Myths [278 words]	78
12	Adventure		Planning your reading	My Australian Adventure [306 words]	84
Review 4			Review of Reading Strategies 10–12 Corporal Punishment in U.S. Schools [375 words]		90
Vocabulary Index					94

1 Personality

Warm Up

1 Each adjective in the box describes a personality trait. Match one with each picture.

Personality Traits			
hard-working	intelligent	energetic/active	serious
humorous/funny	outgoing/friendly	shy/quiet	calm
kind/caring	honest/sensitive	creative	adventurous

A _____ B _____ C _____

D _____ E _____ F _____

2 What type of personality do you have? Circle your three main traits.

Notes personality：性格　trait：特徴

Reading Strategy: Making hypotheses (Guessing)

Good readers make guesses about the text before they read. This is called **making hypotheses**. Before you read a text, look at the title, the headings, pictures, and the whole text quickly. Then make hypotheses about:

- the topic of the text.
- the opinions the writer will have.
- how the text will make you feel.

While you read, you can check your hypotheses and change them if necessary. You can also make new hypotheses.
This reading strategy will help you understand more as you read, and remember more when you finish reading.

Notes hypothesis：仮説　guessing：推測

Strategy in Focus

1 Look at the title and photos. What do you think the article is about? Choose the best answer.
   a. The unusual personality traits of these famous people.
   b. How these famous people celebrate their birthdays.
   c. The typical personalities of people born under these star signs.

Personality and Star Sign
DL 02 / CD 02

Gwen Stefani: born 3 October 1969, star sign = Libra

The singer Gwen Stefani is a Libran. People born under this sign are usually outgoing and enjoy working with other people. They are usually creative and attractive. People born under the Libra sign are usually happy and sensitive.

© Charles Sykes / Invision / AP / アフロ

2 Read the first and second sentence of the above text. Decide if you want to change your hypothesis.

Feedback:
The best answer is c. Some people in the West believe that your star sign influences your personality.

3 Look at the title of the following texts. What do you think they will be about? Choose the best answer.
   a. The personality traits of people born under the Aquarius and Cancer star signs.
   b. The personal traits of Oprah Winfrey and Lindsay Lohan.
   c. The life of Oprah Winfrey and Lindsay Lohan.

Oprah Winfrey: born 29 January 1954, star sign = Aquarius

DL 03 / CD 03

The TV talk-show host Oprah Winfrey is an Aquarius. People born under this sign are usually intelligent and honest. People born under this sign also care about other people very much. They think it is important that everyone is treated fairly.

© Everett Collection / アフロ

Lindsay Lohan: born 2 July 1986, star sign = Cancer

DL 04 / CD 04

The actress Lindsay Lohan was born under the sign of Cancer. These people are usually very sensitive. They don't hide their feelings so it is easy to see if they are happy, sad, or angry. If you were born under this sign, you are probably very kind and like to have very close friends.

© Splash / アフロ

Feedback:
The correct answer is a. These two texts clearly come from the article *Personality* and *Star Sign*, as the texts contain similar information.

Notes unusual：まれな、珍しい　typical：典型的な、特有の　star sign：（十二宮の）星座（sign of zodiac とも言う）　Libra：てんびん座　influence：影響する　Aquarius：みずがめ座　fairly：平等に　Cancer：かに座　contain：含む、持っている　similar：よく似た、類似した

Reading Your Music and Your Personality

▶▶ Before Reading

❶ How do you make a hypothesis? Circle the statements you think are correct.

   a. Read and understand every word in the text.
   b. Read the title and guess what the text is about.
   c. Look at the pictures and guess what the text is about.
   d. Look at the whole text quickly and guess what it is about.

❷ Look at the title of the text on the opposite page. What do you think the text is about? (Make a hypothesis.) Choose the best answer.

   a. How listening to music changes your personality.
   b. How you choose music according to your mood.
   c. How your taste in music can identify your personality.
   d. How people copy the personality traits of their favorite musicians.

▶▶ While Reading

❸ Read the first paragraph of the text. Then decide if you want to change your hypothesis (Question 2) to, one of the following:

   a. A married couple called Jim and Sue.
   b. A punk rock band called the New York Dolls.
   c. How listening to music changes your personality.
   d. How your taste in music can identify your personality.

❹ Continue reading the text and check your hypothesis.

▶▶ After Reading

❺ Decide if these statements are true (T) or false (F), according to the text.

   a. T F Sue and Jim dated for five years before they got married.
   b. T F You can tell more about people from their clothes than their taste in music.
   c. T F Fans of classical music are shy and fans of rap are quiet.
   d. T F People who like the same type of music often have similar personality traits.

❻ Read the text again. Find the personality traits for each type of music:

   a. punk rock _____   b. rock and pop _____

   c. heavy metal / rap _____   d. classical _____

   e. jazz _____   f. hip-hop _____

Your Music and Your Personality

[1] Sue and Jim were neighbors for five years but they were never interested in each other. Then one day, Sue saw Jim's music collection. She noticed a rare punk rock CD that she also owned. At that moment, she realized that they both shared the same interest in music and they started talking. Sue said, "I thought we had nothing in common until I saw his CD by the New York Dolls." They are now married and living with each other.

[2] Some psychologists believe that your taste in music is related to your personality. As part of a test at the University of Texas, Austin, USA, volunteers created a CD of their favorite songs. The volunteers then listened to each other's CDs and made guesses about the CD creator's personality—outgoing, adventurous, happy, and so on. These strangers correctly guessed much more about each others' personalities through their CDs than through their clothes or taste in films. For example, Sue and Jim love punk music, which means they have outgoing personalities.

[3] The psychologists who carried out the test found Snoop Dogg (hip-hop) fans are likely to be energetic and talkative. People who like U2 (rock/pop music) are generally independent and adventurous.

[4] The psychologists also found that Louis Armstrong (jazz) fans tend to be serious and intelligent while fans of classical music are also likely to enjoy jazz music and tend to be shy. The psychologists were surprised to find that rap and heavy metal fans were also shier and quieter than many other music lovers.

(256 words)

Notes neighbor：隣人 rare：まれな、珍しい punk rock：パンクロック（1970年代に英国などで流行した過激なロックミュージックの一種） own：[動] 所有する、持っている have nothing in common：共通して持っているものは何もない psychologist：心理学者 taste：趣味 stranger：見知らぬ人 carry out：実行する、おこなう hip-hop：ヒップホップ（1980年代に米国などで流行した音楽の一種） talkative：おしゃべりな independent：独立した、独立心の強い rap（= rap music）：ラップ（1970年代に米国の黒人文化で流行した音楽のスタイル）

▍Word Work

❼ Correct the mistakes in these words chunks, without looking at the the text.

a. Sue and Jim were neighbors for five years, but they were never **interested in some other**.

_____

b. She realized that they both **shared the same hobby in music** and they started talking.

_____

c. "I thought we had **nothing in similar** until I saw a CD by the New York Dolls."

_____

d. Sue and Jim are now **married and living each other**.

_____

OUTPUT! Writing & Speaking

It is often said that a person's blood type (i.e., A, B, AB, O) is predictive of his/her personality. What personality traits do you think people of each blood type have? Write your ideas and tell them to your partner. Discuss if you do not agree with your partner.

a. I think people with **A** blood type are usually

_____

b. I think people with **B** blood type are usually

_____

c. I think people with **AB** blood type are usually

_____

d. I think people with **O** blood type are usually

_____

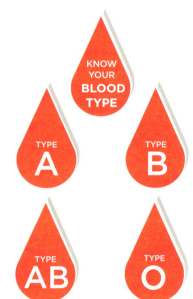

Notes   be predictive of ~ : ～を予測する

2 Happiness

Warm Up

How happy are you? Take the happiness test. Then score your answers.

Are You Happy?

1. When your teacher gives you a leaflet, you:
   a. say thank you.
   b. nod your head.
   c. say nothing.

2. How often do you send instant messages (IM)?
   a. never.
   b. sometimes.
   c. all the time.

3. When shopping for a new cell phone, you:
   a. buy it right away.
   b. wait and think about it.
   c. look for the best deal.

4. You would rather buy:
   a. a bike, a skateboard, or ticket to a game/concert.
   b. a TV, video game, or stereo.
   c. an expensive watch, jewelry, or designer clothes.

Give yourself 3 points for every a, 2 points for every b and 1 point for every c.
9–12 points: You have the secret of happiness—please share!
5–8 points: You probably have good and bad days but you are probably happy.
1–4 points: You tend to feel blue.

Feedback:
1. Saying "thank you" is a quick and easy way to develop relationships.
2. According to studies, people who communicate with their friends on the phone or in person are happier than people who use IM.
3. Unhappy people often find it difficult to make decisions.
4. Spending money on experiences makes people happier than buying goods.

Notes leaflet：(広告の) ちらし、リーフレット   nod：うなずく   spend：(お金や時間を) 費やす

Reading Strategy: Skimming

Good readers usually look at a text quickly before they start reading carefully. This is called **skimming**.

You can skim a text in different ways. You can read:

- the title and other headings, and look at the pictures.
- the first sentence of each paragraph.
- the last sentence of each paragraph.

If you do not have time to read the text carefully, you can use several skimming methods to understand it.
Skimming helps you understand the main idea of the text before reading it carefully. **Skimming** can also help you decide if you need or want to read the whole text.

Notes skim：(本などを) 飛ばし読みする、ざっと読む   method：方法

Strategy in Focus

1 Take one minute to skim the text. Look at the title, the pictures, and read the first sentence of each paragraph. What is the main idea of the text?

a. Money doesn't make you happy.
b. Advice to make yourself happier.
c. Ideas for helping other people to be happy.

The Secrets of Happiness

🎧 DL 06
💿 CD 06

Most people want to be happy, but few know how to find happiness. Money and success alone do not bring lasting happiness. Aristotle, a Greek philosopher, said, "Happiness depends upon ourselves." In other words, we make our own happiness. Here are a few suggestions to help you be happier.

The first secret of happiness is to enjoy the simple things in life. Too often, we spend so much time thinking about the future—for example, getting into college or getting a good job—that we fail to enjoy the present. You should enjoy life's simple pleasures, such as reading a good book, listening to your favorite music, or spending time with close friends. People who have several close friends tend to live happier and healthier lives.

Another secret to leading a happy life is to be active, and have hobbies where you forget your problems and lose track of time. Many people experience this dancing, or playing a sport, such as snowboarding or soccer. You can forget about your problems, and only think about the activity.

Finally, many people find happiness in helping others. According to studies, people feel good when they volunteer their time to help others. If you want to feel happier, do something nice for someone. You can help a friend with his or her studies, go shopping to buy food for an elderly relative, or simply help out around the house by washing the dishes.

2 Read the text more carefully and decide if you were correct about its main idea.

Feedback:
The best answer is b. as the text gives many suggestions to find happiness. Answers a. and c. are mentioned only as examples.

Notes　lasting：長続きする　Aristotle：[ǽrəstɑ̀tl]　アリストテレス（古代ギリシアの哲学者）　suggestion：提案、示唆　fail to ...：…しない、…しそびれる　lose track of time：時間がたつのを忘れる　elderly：年配の　relative：親戚

Reading A Businessman's View

▶▶ Before Reading

❶ Take two minutes to skim the story *A Businessman's View*. What is the story about?

    a. A businessman learns how to fish.
    b. A fisherman wants to become a businessman.
    c. A businessman gives advice to a fisherman.

❷ Tell a partner what you think the main idea of the story is.

▶▶ While Reading

❸ Read the story more carefully and check your hypothesis.

▶▶ After Reading

❹ Ask a partner these questions about the text.

    a. What do you think makes the American businessman happy?
    b. What do you think makes the Mexican fisherman happy?
    c. What is a "full and busy life" (paragraph 7) for the businessman, the fisherman, and for you?

❺ Rewrite these sentences so that they are true for the story.

    a. Martin had been going on vacation to the fishing village for a couple of years.

    _____

    b. It took Pablo all day to catch the fish.

    _____

    c. Pablo thinks his life is too busy.

    _____

    d. Martin thinks Pablo can make more money by buying a supermarket.

    _____

    e. When Pablo retires as a millionaire, his lifestyle will be very different.

    _____

A Businessman's View

[1] Martin Lynch, an American businessman, had been going on vacation to a small Mexican fishing village for a number of years. One morning while going for a walk along the beach, he saw his friend Pablo Perez, a local fisherman. Martin watched Pablo unload his boat and pack the fish in a box.

[2] Martin noticed Pablo was smiling and looked very happy. He could also see several large fish in the boat. Martin greeted Pablo and asked how long it took to catch the fish.

[3] "Just a few hours," replied Pablo.

[4] Martin asked, "Why didn't you stay longer and catch more fish."

[5] "I have enough for my family," Pablo said.

[6] "And what do you do with the rest of your day?" asked Martin.

[7] "I take a nap, play with my children, spend time with my wife, and go into the village to see my friends and play cards. I have a full and busy life."

[8] Martin explained that if Pablo worked longer hours and caught more fish, he could make more money. With the extra money, Pablo could buy more boats and catch many more fish. By selling the fish, Pablo could open his own factory and sell direct to supermarkets.

[9] "Then what?" asked Pablo.

[10] "Well you would probably have to move to Mexico City to run the business. Eventually, you would be able to sell your business and make millions of dollars," replied Martin.

[11] "How long will that take?" asked Pablo.

[12] Martin thought for a while and said it would probably take at least 15 years.

[13] "And then what?" asked Pablo.

[14] "Well, that's the best part," Martin said. "You will be able to retire, buy a house near the ocean, sleep longer, play with your children, spend more time with your wife, see your friends, and play cards."

(303 words)

Notes　local：地元の、現地の　unload：(積荷を)おろす　the rest of ~：~の残り　nap：昼寝　extra：余分な、余った　eventually：結局は、ついに　for a while：しばらくの間　retire：退職する

Word Work

6 Complete the word chunks using the verbs in the box. You can use some of the verbs more than once.

| run | stay | go | spend | catch | make | take |

a. _____ on vacation

b. _____ for a walk

c. _____ the fish

d. _____ longer

e. _____ the business

f. _____ more money

g. _____ time with

h. _____ a nap

OUTPUT! Writing & Speaking

How do you think Pablo responds to Martin after paragraph 14? And what does Martin say to Pablo? Write at least four more sentences of the dialogue to continue the story. When finished, share your ideas with your partner.

_____

_____

_____

_____

_____

_____

_____

3 Friendship

Warm Up

1 What qualities are most important in a best friend? Rank the qualities: ✓✓ = very important, ✓ = important, ✗ = not important. Tell a partner about your ideas.

a. _____ sense of humor   b. _____ same interests   c. _____ popularity

d. _____ kindness   e. _____ honesty   f. _____ intelligence

2 Take the friendship test.

The Friendship Test

❶ Do you remember your best friend's birthday?
   ○ Yes   ○ No

❷ Would you lend your friend your favorite CD?
   ○ Yes   ○ No

❸ Would you help your best friend cheat in an exam?
   ○ Yes   ○ No

❹ You are about to leave your house to see your favorite band in concert. Your friend phones because his girlfriend/her boyfriend has broken up with him/her. Your friend wants to meet you and talk. Do you go to your friend and miss the concert?
   ○ Yes   ○ No

Notes　cheat：［動］だます、（試験で）カンニングをする　break up：（関係や友情が）終わる、（友人や恋人と）別れる

Reading Strategy: Scanning

Sometimes it is a good idea to **scan** a text before reading it carefully. When you **scan**, you look over the text very quickly looking for the information you need.

When you **scan** a text, you look for peoples' names, places, numbers, dates, and times, as well as other key words.

Scanning helps you find information quickly without reading the whole text. **Scanning** can also help you make a hypothesis about the text.

Notes　scan：（新聞など、必要な情報を得るために）ざっと読む

Strategy in Focus

1 Take three minutes to scan each advertisement. Complete the following information:

	Name	Age	Nationality	Wants	Where
a.	Nora	___	___	e-Pals	Asia, Japan, Korea, Taiwan
b.	Patrick	___	___	___	___
c.	Steve	___	___	___	___

Looking for Friends 🎧 DL 08 💿 CD 08

a. Looking for e-Pals (email pen pals)

My name is Nora, and I want to make friends with people in other countries and learn about other cultures. I am 18 years old and I go to college in Quebec, Canada. I like to snowboard in the winter and hike in the Rocky Mountains during the summer. I enjoy listening to all types of music, but at the moment I like Beyoncé, Christina Aguilera, and Kanye West. I am very interested in Asia, and would like to make friends with students in Japan, Korea, or Taiwan. Please email me if you would like a Canadian e-pal.

b. Looking for Homestay Family

My name is Patrick, I'm 17 and have just finished high school in Australia. I'll be traveling around the world for a year before I start university. I will be in South and Central America from September to February, and in Asia from March to August. I can exchange English and surfing lessons for a place to stay. I would prefer to stay with a family for two to four weeks at a time. Please email me if I can stay with your family.

c. Language Exchange

I am Steve, and I am a 30-year-old American businessman. I often travel to Spain, France, and Italy, and spend three months in each country every year. I would like to know more people and learn the language while I am in these countries. If you help me learn your language I can teach you English and about American culture, or I can pay for a meal. Email me if you are interested.

Feedback:
Key words (e-Pals, Homestay, and Language Exchange) in the title of each advertisement tell you what each person wants. Capital letters are used for names of people and places, as well as months and nationalities. Numbers for example, for ages, are easy to see in a text.

Notes advertisement：広告、宣伝　nationality：国籍　Quebec：ケベック（カナダ東部の州）　the Rocky Mountains：ロッキー山脈（北米大陸のカナダからアメリカ合衆国に走る山脈）　at the moment：今のところ　Beyoncé：ビヨンセ（米国のシンガーソングライター、ダンサー、音楽プロデューサー、女優）　Christina Aguilera：クリスティーナ・アギレラ（米国のシンガーソングライター）　Kanye West：カニエ・ウェスト（米国のミュージシャン、音楽プロデューサー、ファッションデザイナー）　capital letter：大文字

2 Scan the advertisements to answer these questions.

a. Which musicians is Nora listening to at the moment? _____

b. Where will Patrick be from March to August? _____

c. How much time does Steve spend in Spain every year? _____

3 Now read the texts. Decide who you would email.

Reading What I Like Most About My Best Friend

▶▶ **Before Reading**

❶ Scan the texts to complete the information below.

Name	Nationality	Best Friend's Name	Best Friend's Personality Traits
a. Lilly Chen	_____	_____	_____
b. Alan Cordoba	_____	_____	_____
c. Isabel Famosa	_____	_____	_____
d. Ken Ichigawa	_____	_____	_____

▶▶ **While Reading**

❷ As you read the text, underline any statements that are true for you and your bestfriend.

▶▶ **After Reading**

❸ Ask a partner these questions about the text.

a. Whose best friend do you like most? Why?
b. What personality traits do you like most?

❹ Decide if the statements are true (T) or false (F), according to the text.

a. T F May and Lilly are good friends because they have similar personalities.
b. T F Fanny is a caring person.
c. T F Isabel and Ana both live in Cuba.
d. T F Ken doesn't like Daisuke's jokes.

❺ Circle the adjective that is NOT true for each best friend.

a. May is:	confident	kind	shy
b. Fanny is:	intelligent	calm	interesting
c. Ana is:	serious	honest	kind
d. Daisuke is:	funny	quiet	talkative

What I Like Most About My Best Friend

Lilly Chen, Taiwan

[1] May is the most confident girl that I have ever met. Although she looks tough, she is really kind. It may surprise some people to find out that May and I are best friends, because we have very different personalities. I lack confidence and I am quite shy, which is the opposite of May but I think this is why we are such good friends.

Alan Cordoba, Mexico

[2] My best friend is Fanny, my girlfriend. I can always depend on her. We always take care of each other. The first week we met, I got sick with flu and she came to my house to take care of me every day. She is also very intelligent and interesting, although sometimes she gets angry. She yells at me for always being late.

Isabel Famosa, Cuba

[3] My best friend is Ana Hernandez. She is honest, kind, and sensitive. We were born in the same city in Cuba. We spent a lot of time together until we were 12. Then, I moved to America with my family and I thought I would never see Ana again. When I went to college in New York, Ana had a room in the same dormitory. She now lives near me in New Jersey and we see each other all the time.

Ken Ichigawa, Japan

[4] I love to spend time with Daisuke because he makes me laugh so much. He's very funny. We share the same sense of humor, and know how to make each other cry with laughter. We enjoy talking about the funny things we did when we were children, and tell the same stupid jokes over and over again.

(278 words)

Notes confident：自信のある　tough：頑強な、丈夫な、(生活などが) 困難な　lack：〜を欠いている、持っていない　flu：流感、インフルエンザ　yell：大声をあげる、怒鳴る　dormitory：寮 (略式 dorm)　stupid：馬鹿げた　over and over (again)：何度も繰り返して

Word Work

6 Circle the correct word chunk.

a. Fanny and Alan have a good relationship because they always **take over each other / take care of each other** when they are sick.

b. Alan's girlfriend **gets angry / has angry** when he is late.

c. Ken prefers to **do time / spend time** with his friends than study.

d. Ken and Daisuke enjoy telling the same jokes and stories **over and under again / over and over again**.

e. Most people share a **sense of humor / feeling of humor** with their best friends.

OUTPUT! Writing & Speaking

Think about one of your close friends. Write a short description about the thing you like the most about him/her. You can use expressions in the reading. When finish, read it to your partner.

_____

_____

_____

_____

_____

_____

_____

_____

Review 1

Review of Reading Strategies

- Unit 1: Making hypotheses
- Unit 2: Skimming
- Unit 3: Scanning

1 Which reading strategies do these sentences describe? Read each statement and check [✓] the best answer.

	Making Hypotheses	Skimming	Scanning
a. Read the title and guess what the text is about.			
b. Only look for information you need.			
c. Look at the picture(s) and guess what the text is about.			
d. Look at the whole text quickly.			
e. Look for dates and numbers.			
f. Read the first sentence of each paragraph.			
g. Look for people's names and place names.			
h. Read the last sentence of each paragraph.			

2 Look at the photos and the title of the article on the opposite page, and make hypotheses. What do you think the article is about? Check [✓] one or more answers.

The article will describe Jennifer Lopez's:

a. _____ family   b. _____ jewelry   c. _____ clothes

d. _____ career   e. _____ life

3 Skim the text to check your hypotheses.

4 Scan the text for names, dates, and places. Answer these questions.

a. When was Jennifer Lopez born?   _____

b. Where was Jennifer Lopez born?   _____

c. When did Jennifer Lopez make her first movies?   _____

d. When did she marry Marc Anthony?   _____

Reading ▶ Jennifer Lopez

[1] Jennifer Lynn Lopez (also known as J.Lo) is a well-known Puerto Rican-American actress and singer. Born July 24, 1970 she was raised in the Bronx area of New York City. Lopez speaks English and Spanish, and has two sisters, Leslie (a music teacher) and Lynda (a TV news presenter).

[2] Before becoming a famous celebrity, Lopez began her career as a backup dancer. She later took up acting, saying that she always wanted to do this.

[3] She started her acting career early in the 1990s with movies like *Mi Familia* and *Money Train*, but she became famous with the movie *Selena*. She followed this with *Out Of Sight*, a movie that also starred George Clooney. Since then she has appeared in many movies, including *The Wedding Planner*, *Enough*, *Maid in Manhattan*, *Shall We Dance*, and *Monster-In-Law*.

[4] J.Lo's music, mainly pop, includes the albums *J.Lo* and *On The 6*, a reference to the subway line she used to take growing up in the Bronx. In the fall of 2002, Lopez released *This Is Me ... Then*, an album which included three hugely popular singles: *Jenny From The Block*, *All I Have* (one of 2003's most popular songs), and *I'm Glad*. On November 18, 2003, she released her fifth album, *Reel Me*.

[5] On June 5, 2004, Lopez married singer Marc Anthony, who is also a Puerto Rican from New York.

[6] Since being married, the couple has often sung together, and in 2006 they acted

© Broadimage /アフロ

together in the movie *El Cantante*.

[7] This was not Lopez's first marriage, actually it is her third and Anthony's second.

[8] Lopez's first marriage, which was with Ojani Noa, ended in divorce in 1998 after just 21 months, and her second marriage, which was with Chris Judd, her former backup dancer, only lasted from 2001 to 2002. Between her first two marriages, Lopez dated the singer and designer Puff Daddy, breaking up after a shooting incident in a New York nightclub. She then dated and was engaged to the actor Ben Affleck, but their marriage, planned for September 13, 2003, was called off a few days before the wedding. In January 2004 the couple split.

(355 words)

Notes celebrity：（芸能界などの）有名人　backup dancer：（うしろで踊る）ダンサー　take up：取りかかる、始める　star：［動］主演させる　a reference to ～：～について語ったもの　hugely：大いに、非常に　divorce：離婚、離婚する　date：［動］デート（交際）する　［名］交際相手　shooting：発砲　be engaged to ～：～と婚約する　call off：（予定などを）中止する、取り消す　split：別れる、破局を迎える

Comprehension Check

1 Decide if the statements are true (T) or false (F), according to the article.
   a. T F   Jennifer Lopez was born in Puerto Rico.
   b. T F   Jennifer Lopez was an actress before she took up singing.
   c. T F   Jennifer Lopez has been married three times.
   d. T F   Jennifer Lopez married Ben Affleck on September 13, 2003.

2 The word "this" at the end of the second paragraph refers to:
   a. singing   b. dancing   c. acting   d. becoming famous

3 According to the article, Jennifer Lopez:
   a. always wanted to act with George Clooney.
   b. decided to be an actress in the early 1990s.
   c. wanted to be a backup dancer for a long time.
   d. didn't appear in a lot of movies in the 1990s.

4 The word "incident" in the final paragraph is closest in meaning to:
   a. game   b. fight   c. festival   d. practice

5 According to the text, which statement about Jennifer Lopez is NOT true?
   a. Jennifer Lopez and her first husband divorced after less than two years of marriage.
   b. Jennifer Lopez's second husband was one of her backup dancers.
   c. Jennifer Lopez was engaged to Puff Daddy and Ben Affleck before she married Marc Anthony.
   d. Both Marc Anthony and Jennifer Lopez have been married before.

More Word Chunks

Complete the sentences, using these word chunks from Units 1, 2 and 3.

| over again | interests | humor | common | go on | time | business |

   a. My best friend is very funny. He has a good **sense of** _____ and makes me laugh a lot.

   b. This summer I want to _____ **vacation** to Kyoto in Japan.

   c. My friend has his own Internet company. He **runs the** _____ from home.

   d. I am very busy during the week, but on the weekend I like to **spend** _____ **with** my friends and family.

   e. I hate that song. I heard it **over and** _____ on the radio this summer.

   f. Jennifer Lopez and Marc Anthony **share the same** _____ **in** singing and acting.

   g. Often married couples who **have nothing in** _____ end up getting divorced.

26 • Review 1

OUTPUT! Speaking

Scanning is very useful when we need specific information such as a word in the dictionary, a restaurant in the telephone book, and the sales items in the advertisement. Look at the TV guide below. Your teacher will ask you questions about TV programs on the guide. Scan the guide to find the information asked as soon as possible.

Notes specific：ある特定の   item：商品、項目

SBC 1	SBC 2	SBC 3	SBC 4
19:00 Hi! Celebrity A complete biography of Jennifer Lopez, as a singer, a dancer, and an actress.	**19:00 A True Hero** Episode 7: Karl saved his enemy, Sancho, from falling off the cliff.	**19:00 Smart Rover** A tale of adventures of a dog, Rover, and four children, who found a secret place in the woods.	**19:00 SBC News and Regional News** The latest national and local news stories from the SBC, followed by the weather.
19:30 The Oprah Winfrey Show Oprah surprises her mom presenting her favorite chicken pie.	**19:30 One Piece** Luffy loses his shadow power while battling the Oars and the Straw Hats try to help.	**19:30 As Seen on TV** Best sellers 2014-17, with items buy one get one free campaign.	**19:30 High School Now** A teacher, Vanessa Perez, reports on the recent high school education.
20:00 The World Angler The documentary of a local fisher man, Pablo Perez, living in a small Mexican village.	**20:00 Mean Girls** Starring Lindsay Lohan, describing female high school students criticizing each other.	**20:00 Good Money** Financial specialist Martin Lynch offers his insights into the market.	**20:00 Scientific Facts** Psychologist Dan Williams reviews the latest study about human personality traits.
21:00 SBC Nightly News Find more about SBC Nightly News.		**20:30 SportsCenter at SBC** Baseball, soccer, hockey, football, etc. sports of the day.	**20:30 Kuu Kuu Harajuku** Gwen Stefani's animated kids show based on Japanese street culture.

Reading: Jennifer Lopez • 27

4 Difficult Decisions

Warm Up

1 Guess what difficult decision these friends are making.

2 Read the following text. Do you think the friends made the right decision?

After eating dinner at a restaurant, Sunni and her friends got the bill and noticed that the server forgot to charge them for drinks and dessert. They decided not to say anything. The dinner was expensive and it was the server's mistake.

Notes bill：請求書　server：給仕する人（レストランのウェイターなど）　charge：（支払いを）請求する

Reading Strategy: Making predictions

Good readers make **predictions** while they are reading. They think about what action, topic, or words will come next.

For example, "I was on vacation in Hong Kong, and I couldn't believe it when I saw ..." How do you think this sentence will end?

If you predicted the sentence ends with "Jackie Chan," or "my friend from school," you would be making a good prediction.

Making and checking **predictions** while you are reading will help you understand and stay interested in the text.

Notes prediction：予測

Strategy in Focus

1 What do you think is happening in the picture? Make predictions. You can say your predictions either in English or in Japanese.

2 Now read the text. Predict what the writer says to his girlfriend.

It was my birthday last week and my girlfriend gave me a sweater. It was not my taste at all. She asked me if I liked it, and I said, ...

a. "Why didn't you give me money?"
b. "Not really. Can we take it back to the store tomorrow?"
c. "Of course I do. It's great."

3 What do you think is happening in the picture? Make predictions. You can say your predictions either in English or in Japanese.

4 Now read the text. Predict what the writer tells Chiya.

My friend Chiya spent all night working on an English paper and didn't have time to do her math homework. She asked me if it was OK to copy my homework. I told her ...

Feedback:

Activity 2. The correct prediction is probably c. Many people think it is polite to thank someone for a gift even if they don't like it. You can use your own experience of giving and receiving gifts to make this prediction.

Activity 4. Possible predictions are:

- she should do the homework by herself. She will not learn by copying.
- just this time. But never again. I don't want to get caught.
- to ask another friend. I don't think it is right to copy.

It is important that you make predictions when you read. It is also important to understand if your prediction was correct. Making predictions helps you enjoy and focus on the text.

Reading Choosing the Right Career

▶▶ Before Reading

❶ What could help you choose a career? Choose one or more answers.

- **a.** Think about what you enjoy doing.
- **b.** Do an internship at a company.
- **c.** Listen to music to relax you.
- **d.** Read about different careers.
- **e.** Think about what's important to you in life.
- **f.** Talk to people about their jobs.

❷ You will read these sentences in the text. Predict which ending matches the beginning of each sentence.

- **a.** If you follow these three steps,
- **b.** Before you decide upon a career,
- **c.** Also, talk to people already doing jobs that you find interesting,
- **d.** Most people change jobs several times during their work life,

- **i.** think about your interests, and your talents and values, and then think about jobs that fit them.
- **ii.** so don't put too much pressure on yourself to make the perfect decision.
- **iii.** you'll have a good chance of finding a career that will keep you interested for a long time.
- **iv.** and try out careers by taking internships or part-time jobs.

▶▶ While Reading

❸ As you read the text, check your predictions.

▶▶ After Reading

❹ Ask a partner these questions about the text.

- **a.** Do you agree with the author's advice on how to choose a career?
- **b.** What else would you recommend?

❺ According to the article, when should you ask these questions? Number them in the order in which they appear in the text.

- **a.** What kind of qualifications do I require to get this job? _____
- **b.** What do I enjoy doing? _____
- **c.** Is monthly salary more important to me than time off? _____
- **d.** What do I do well? _____
- **e.** Do I like working with people or working by myself? _____
- **f.** How much does this job pay? _____

Choosing the Right Career

[1] For many students, choosing a career is the most important life decision they must make at school. But, choosing the right career is not easy. So how do you find one that you will enjoy and find satisfying?

[2] If you follow these three steps, you will have a good chance of finding a career that will keep you interested for a long time.

Step One: Reflection

[3] Before you decide upon a career, think about your interests and your talents, and then think about jobs that fit them. Ask yourself: What do I enjoy doing? What do I do well? Then think about the jobs that match these interests and talents.

Step Two: Planning

[4] Next, learn about your career options. See if the library has books describing different kinds of work, the typical qualifications required, and the typical salaries for various jobs. Also, talk to people already doing jobs that you find interesting, and try out careers by taking internships or part-time jobs.

Step Three: Selection

[5] After you have spent time on steps one and two, consider what kind of personality you have and what your values are: what is important to you. Perhaps you like working face to face with people. If so, a job as a computer programmer may not be the best option. If you like the security of getting a monthly salary, then starting your own business probably is not for you.

[6] Finally, remember that you can always change your mind. Most people change jobs several times during their working life, so do not put too much pressure on yourself to make the perfect decision right now. Your first job right after college probably will not be your career thirty years from now. Be flexible and allow yourself to change if you are not satisfied with your chosen career.

(304 words)

Notes satisfy：満足させる　reflection：熟考（すること）　talent：才能　option：選択肢　qualification：資格、免許　require：必要とする　try out：試してみる　internship：インターン、職業研修　consider：よく考える　value：価値、価値観　security：安全、安心、安定　flexible：融通のきく、柔軟な　allow：許す

Word Work

6 Complete the sentences using the word chunks below.

| be flexible | changed her mind | put too much pressure on |
| several times | right after | |

a. After changing jobs _____, I eventually found a job that I really liked.

b. I was lucky: I found a job _____ leaving school.

c. Parents and teachers tend to _____ youngsters to pass the university entrance exam and get a good job.

d. You should _____ and change your job if you are unhappy at work.

e. Sarah wanted to be a doctor, but she _____. Now she wants to go to graduate school to study law.

OUTPUT! Writing & Speaking

Write down your interests, what you enjoy doing, and what you can do well. Then write about your dream job and why you are suitable for the job. After you finish, read them to your partner.

a. My interests: I am interested in _____

b. What I enjoy: I enjoy _____

c. What I can do well: I can _____

d. My dream job: My dream job is _____

e. Why I am suitable for the job: The reason I am suitable for the job is _____

_____

Notes suitable：適している

DREAM JOB

5 Life-Changing Moments

Warm Up

1 Describe the pictures.

A _____   B _____

2 Take one minute to skim the blog entries on the next page. Then write the name of the writer under the correct picture in activity 1.

> Notes   blog entry：コンピュータのブログ記事

Reading Strategy: Making inferences

To **make an inference**, you read a text, sentence, or phrase, think about it, and understand things about the text that are not mentioned.

For example, after reading, "Suzy is relaxing on her sofa." you can infer:

- Suzy is a woman; Suzy is a woman's name and the writer uses "her" to refer to Suzy.
- Suzy is probably at home; we usually find sofas in homes and we know that it is Suzy's sofa.
- Suzy is probably lying down on her sofa; many people lie down when relaxing on their sofa.

The writer doesn't tell us that Suzy is a woman who is lying on her sofa at home, but we can make these inferences from the information in the text.

Your **inferences** help you understand the text and the author better.

> Notes   inference：[ínfərəns] 推測   infer：[infə́ːr] 推測する   lie down：横になる

34 · 5: Life-Changing Moments

Strategy in Focus

Read Vanessa and Min-ho's blog entries. Check [✓] the inferences you can make.

a. _____ Vanessa's parents are rich.
b. _____ When Vanessa was young, she was often sick.
c. _____ Vanessa thinks reading improved her grades.
d. _____ Min-ho is hard working.
e. _____ Min-ho always wanted to be a travel agent.
f. _____ Going to China was a positive experience for Min-ho.

When I was seven years old, I caught the flu and stayed home from school. My parents had to work, so my neighbor came over to look after me. She read to me for hours and it felt like I was listening to a movie. She started my interest in reading. I was never a good student, but my grades started improving at school. When I graduate next spring, I have a job teaching English to high school students.

Vanessa Perez, San Francisco, the United States

I was a quiet student at high school and spent most of my time studying. I needed to get good grades and get into a good college. After college, I realized I had no idea what I wanted to do next and I didn't have any real friends. I worked in a restaurant for the summer and saved enough money to go to China for two months. I came back changed. While traveling, I had learned some Chinese and made friends from all over the world as well as China. Some of them are coming to visit me next summer.

Min-ho Lee, Pusan, South Korea

© TonyV3112 / Shutterstock.com

Feedback:

The correct answers are c. d. and f.

c. We can infer that Vanessa thinks reading improved her grades because she says before she was interested in reading she wasn't a good student. Now that she is interested in reading, her grades are better.

d. We can infer Min-ho is hard-working because he says he spent most of his time studying in high school and he worked during his summer holiday in a restaurant to save money to travel.

f. We can infer that Min-ho had a positive experience because he says he changed and now has friends that will visit him in Korea and he speaks some Chinese.

Notes improve：向上させる、よくする　positive：前向きの、プラス（思考）の

Reading Ana and Her Fiancé

▶▶ Before Reading

❶ Look at the title of the text and picture. Decide what you think the story is about.

   a. A woman who broke up with her fiancé.
   b. A woman who always argued with her fiancé.
   c. A woman who was desperate to see her fiancé.

❷ Scan the text to match the character with correct description.

| Ana's old friend | who had loved Ana | a tough businessman who owned a boat |
| Ana's fiancé | Ana's younger brother | a tragic heroine of the story |

   Character   Description
   a. Ana   _____
   b. Ken   _____
   c. Marc   _____
   d. Ethan   _____
   e. Daniel   _____

▶▶ While Reading

❸ As you read the story, check your answers to questions 1 and 2.

▶▶ After Reading

❹ Talk about the people in the story with a partner.

   a. I think the story is ...
   b. I think Ana was right/wrong because...
   c. I think Ken was right/wrong because...
   d. I like (name) the most because...
   e. I dislike (name) the most because...

❺ Choose one personality trait for each character in the story. There are a number of possible answers. Discuss your answers with a partner.

friendly	selfish	hard-working	jealous	talkative	shy
energetic	honest	humorous	serious	intelligent	independent
sensitive	kind	adventurous	calm		

   a. Ana   _____
   b. Ken   _____
   c. Marc   _____
   d. Ethan   _____
   e. Daniel _____

36 • 5: Life-Changing Moments

Ana and Her Fiancé

[1] Ana, a beautiful young country girl from a poor family, lived near a wide and dangerous river in the jungle. The river was known for its crocodiles and fast-moving water. On the other side of the river lived Ana's fiancé, Ken. He was working hard to save money for their wedding, and Ana had not seen Ken for six months.

[2] Ana was feeling very lonely without Ken and was desperate to see him. She asked Marc to take her across the river in his boat. Marc, who was a very tough businessman, said it would cost Ana $800. She did not have that much money and would not be able to save it in years. She begged Marc to take her across the river in his boat. Finally, Marc said he would take Ana if she worked for him for two months.

[3] Ana knew Ken did not like Marc and she did not know what to do. She asked her younger brother, Ethan, for help. She explained her situation to Ethan but he said it was not his problem and she needed to decide for herself.

[4] Ana was very upset and even more desperate to see her fiancé. She was so in love with Ken she would do anything to see him, so she agreed to work for Marc.

[5] After two months, Marc took Ana across the river to Ken. They were both very happy and excited to see each other. Before long, Ken asked Ana how she had crossed the river. Ana told him the truth and Ken became very angry. He told Ana that he would not marry her. Ana crossed the river again and went home heartbroken.

[6] When Ana returned home, she met an old friend, Daniel. She told Daniel her sad story. Daniel looked at Ana with a smile and said, "Ana, I have always loved you. I will marry you."

(315 words)

Notes crocodile：クロコダイル（大型のワニ）　fiancé：フィアンセ（女性から見た婚約者）　desperate：（何かを）切望してやまない　beg：請う、懇願する　upset：取り乱した　before long：まもなく　heartbroken：深く傷ついた、悲しみに満ちた

Word Work

❻ Complete the word chunks according to the story.

a. **On the other side of the** _____ lived Ana's fiancé, Ken.

b. Ana was feeling very lonely without Ken and **was desperate to** _____ him.

c. Ana **did not know what to** _____, so she turned to her brother, Ethan, for help.

d. She was so in love with him, she **would do** _____ **to see him**.

OUTPUT! Writing

Write a letter from the viewpoint of Ana to Ken or from Ken to Ana after they broke up. In the letter, you should explain:

a. how you are feeling now,
b. why you chose to do what you did (Ana chose to work for Marc, and Ken chose to break up with Ana), and
c. what you are going to do now.

> Notes   viewpoint：観点、立場

Dear

6 Unexpected Events

Warm Up

1 Look at the two pictures and predict what will happen next.

　　a. The man gives the woman a reward.
　　b. The woman keeps the wallet for herself.

2 Now read the text and check your prediction.

The woman hands the wallet back to the man and receives $20 as a reward. Unfortunately, she drops her reward on her way back home.

Notes　reward：報酬、ほうび　wallet：財布（札入れ）　drop：落とす

Reading Strategy: Interpreting

To read effectively, you often need to **interpret** the text. Ask yourself, "What is the waitress saying?" Consider this example:

What does the customer mean by, "You must be joking"? Does he think the waitress is joking? No. You can interpret the customer to mean the bill is very expensive and he wasn't expecting such a large bill.

If you make **interpretations** about the text, you will understand it more fully.

Notes　effectively：効果的に　interpret：[intə́ːrprit] 解釈する（話し手・書き手の意図を読み取る）

Strategy in Focus

1 Read the passage. While reading, decide what the phrase in **bold** means.

   a. She won't be able to remember him.
   b. She will stop hoping to be his girlfriend.
   c. She will forget his name.

Subway Coincidence

Once I was in love with someone who already had a girlfriend. The situation was making me ill so one day, when I was with my friends, I told them, "**I should forget about him.**" I decided that if I ever saw him with his girlfriend, I would do my best to forget about him. Five minutes later we were waiting for a subway train. As we were waiting, the train going in the other direction stopped, and directly in front of me I could see them together on the train holding hands.

Feedback:
The correct answer is b. Men and women often say "I should forget about her/him." when they know the person they love does not love them.

Notes　bold：太字の　coincidence：（偶然の）一致、同時発生　make ~ ill：（人）~をいらいら［むかむか］させる

2 Read the passage. While reading, decide what the sentence in **bold** means.

   a. The writer was too young to realize the meeting was a big coincidence.
   b. The writer was surprised to see Dominic in Egypt.

Chance Meeting

When I was young, my family lived in Thailand because of my father's work. I met and became friends with children from all over the world. One of my friends in Thailand was a boy called Dominic. When I was five, my family returned to England. I said goodbye to all my friends and hoped that we would be able to play together again one day.

My parents decided to take a vacation in Egypt on the way back to England. My father and I were walking around the pyramids when, from around a corner, Dominic and his father appeared. **Because we were only five at the time, neither Dominic nor I found this even slightly odd.** Our dads, of course, were very surprised.

Feedback:
The correct answer is a. The writer is saying that five-year-olds don't understand the great distance between Thailand and Egypt, they didn't realize that seeing each other was a really big coincidence.

Notes　slightly：わずかに、いささか　odd：奇妙な、変わった　distance：距離

Reading A Surprise Gold Medal

▶▶ **Before Reading**

❶ Look at the photo of the sportsman Billy Mills. Read the first and last sentence of each paragraph in the text. Decide if the statements are true (T) or false (F).

a. T F Billy Mills is an Irish American.
b. T F He was one of the fastest runners at his university.
c. T F Everyone expected Billy to win a gold medal.
d. T F Billy was slower than the other runners in the race.
e. T F Billy won an Olympic medal for the 100-meter sprint.

▶▶ **While Reading**

❷ As you read the text, decide what the writer is saying about the following:

a. "Childhood was not easy for Billy." (line 3)
   i. Billy did not have a happy childhood.
   ii. Billy had to study harder than other children.

b. ". . . he lost his mother when he was seven, and his father passed away ..." (lines 4-6)
   i. Both of his parents died.
   ii. His parents divorced and they both left home.

c. "Although he was on the U.S. team, many people did not expect anything from Billy." (lines 23-24)
   i. No one believed he could win a medal.
   ii. Everyone was surprised that Billy was a world record holder.

d. "Everyone else was out of the race ..." (line 37)
   i. The other runners had already finished the race.
   ii. The other runners were far behind.

▶▶ **After Reading**

❸ Ask a partner these questions about the text.

a. Why do you think Billy Mills was able to win the Olympic gold medal?
b. What do you think the writer means when he says, "At first he focused on military life"?
c. Why did nobody think Billy would win the Olympic 10,000-meter medal?

A Surprise Gold Medal

[1] Billy Mills, a Native American, was born and raised on a reservation in the United States. Childhood was not easy for Billy. His family was not well off; he lost his mother when he was seven, and his father passed away five years later. After his father's death, Billy was sent to a boarding school. At school Billy started running to help him forget his problems. To his amazement, he found that he had a talent for running and broke a number of high school records. As a result of his running, he was given an athletic scholarship to the University of Kansas.

[2] At the University of Kansas, Billy continued to win many competitions. After graduation he joined the United States Marine Corps. At first he focused on military life, but he soon returned to running. He did well enough to race in the 1964 Tokyo Olympics in the 10,000 meters and marathon events.

[3] Although he was on the U.S. team, many people did not expect anything from Billy. In the 10,000 meters, Billy was almost a minute slower than the favorite, Ron Clarke of Australia. The other favorite to win the Olympic gold was Mohammad Gammoudi of Tunisia. The rest of the runners included Olympic gold medal and world record

Billy Mills © DOG ROBBER

holders. All eyes were focused on the front runners, not on Billy.

[4] When the race started, everyone was surprised to see Billy Mills at the front with Ron Clarke. For much of the race, the two ran together with Gammoudi just behind them. Everyone else was out of the race, and the crowd expected Mills to tire and slow down.

[5] Near the end of the race, Gammoudi ran between Clarke and Mills and pushed them aside. The two of them almost fell over and Mills dropped behind into third place. However, Mills was determined not to lose. He raced ahead to win the gold, and set an Olympic 10,000 meter record. He was the first Native American to win the Olympic 10,000-meter race.

(334 words)

Notes Native American：アメリカ先住民 reservation：先住民特別保留地 well off：裕福な pass away：死ぬ、亡くなる boarding school：(全寮制の) 寄宿学校 to one's amazement：〜が驚いたことには scholarship：奨学金 competition：競技会 Marine Corps：[məríːn kɔ̀ːr] 海兵隊 military：軍の favorite：優勝候補 crowd：群衆、観衆 fall over：倒れる be determined：決心する

Word Work

❹ Use these word chunks to write sentences about Billy Mills, without looking at the text.

a. born and raised: _____

b. not well off: _____

c. had a talent for: _____

d. As a result of: _____

OUTPUT! Listening & Writing

DL 18
CD 18

You will listen to the summary of "A Surprise Gold Medal" twice. In the first time, just listen to it, and in the second time, you can take notes. Do not try to write every sentence completely, but just write down several words you hear. After the second listening, reproduce the summary with your group member.

MEMO

Notes summary：要約 reproduce：再生する、再び書く

Reading: A Surprise Gold Medal

Review 2

Review of Reading Strategies

- Unit 4: Making predictions
- Unit 5: Making inferences
- Unit 6: Interpreting

1 Which reading strategies do these sentences describe? Read each statement and check [✓] the best answer.

	Making Predictions	Making Inferences	Interpreting
a. Understand things about the text that are not mentioned.	_____	_____	_____
b. Guess what will happen next.	_____	_____	_____
c. Think about what the writer means.	_____	_____	_____
d. Guess what the next word or phrase will be.	_____	_____	_____

2 Read the beginning of the text *Modern Social Networking* below, and predict which words come next. Choose one or more answers.

Throughout history, humans have had an urge to make social connections. Making friends is something that most people do naturally when meeting people through ...

- a. Internet chatrooms
- b. cell phones
- c. family and friends
- d. work or school

3 As you read the text, decide what the writer is saying about the following:

a. "Throughout history, humans have had an urge to make social connections." (paragraph 1)

　i. People have always felt the need to make friends.
　ii. In the past, people felt pressure to make friends.

b. "For many, these sites have made a positive difference in their lives by widening their social circles." (paragraph 4)

　i. Many people have made a lot of new friends because of MySpace.
　ii. Many people go to a lot of parties now because of MySpace.

c. ". . . then changing their mind . . ." (paragraph 4)

　i. They decided not to give them a job.
　ii. They weren't intelligent enough to get a job.

4 Check [✓] the inferences you can make about the text. Underline the words, phrases, or sentences that support your inferences.

a. _____ All the people tend to meet new friends on the Internet rather than through family and friends.

b. _____ Young people don't have much in common with older people.

c. _____ My Space is popular because it is free and has many functions.

d. _____ Some people include negative personal information about themselves on MySpace.

Reading ▶ Modern Social Networking

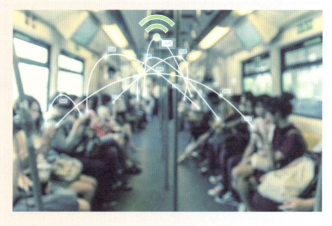

[1] Throughout history, humans have had an urge to make social connections. Making friends is something that most people do naturally when meeting people through family and friends and getting to know people in their neighborhood, at school, or in the workplace. In addition, the Internet has introduced a new meeting place—the social networking site (SNS).

[2] Social networking sites were originally designed to help adults connect with other adults. Users developed their own profile containing personal information (such as likes and dislikes) which others could look through. When you found someone with similar interests to you that you wanted to contact, you posted a message and waited for a reply. These types of SNS were popular but access was usually off limits to children. It should come as no surprise that technologically savvy teenagers would want to use computers in a similar way.

[3] In the United States, MySpace.com is one of the largest social networking sites with over 100 million users. Unlike some sites that require a special invitation to join, MySpace is open to everyone over the age of 14. Users create their own personal profile page and can spend their time blogging, posting photos and instant messaging with other members from all over the world. They can then decide whether they want to make their profile available only to friends or to all registered users.

[4] Many teens now prefer using SNS to stay in touch with friends and meet new people. Instead of asking for a phone number or email address, asking for someone's MySpace profile is becoming a much more popular question. For many, these sites have made a positive difference in their lives by widening their social circles. However, some people have found social networking sites carry some risks. There are stories of employers offering a job and then changing their mind after checking the person's personal profile on the Internet. So be warned—it is important to think about the type of information you include on your profile page.

(334 words)

Notes urge：欲、衝動 in addition：その上、さらに加えて profile：[próufail] プロフィール look through ~：~に目を通す、よく調べる post：掲示する、貼る It should come as no surprise that ~：~は驚くにはあたらない savvy：物知りの（コンピュータ通の） available：入手できる register：登録する stay in touch with ~：~と連絡を取り合う instead of ~：~の代わりに widen：拡げる offer：[動] 提供する、申し出る [名] 申し出 be warned：気をつける

Comprehension Check

1 The word "access" in paragraph 2 is closest in meaning to:

   a. entry   **b.** approach   **c.** route   **d.** exit

2 The phrase "off limits" in paragraph 2 is closest in meaning to:

   a. not available   **b.** out of order   **c.** allowed   **d.** restricted

3 In paragraph 3, the author mentions MySpace.com as an example of:

   a. A social networking site available to all ages.
   b. A social networking site that teenagers over fourteen may use.
   c. A social networking site that employers use.
   d. A social networking site that teenagers have created.

4 In paragraph 4, the author implies that employers use social networking sites to:

   a. Increase the number of staff.   **b.** Fire staff who cause problems at work.
   c. Find new staff.   **d.** Find out if someone is telling the truth.

5 Which of the following is NOT a feature of a social networking site mentioned in the text?

   a. Meeting new people.   **b.** Communicatings with others.
   c. Sharing information about yourself.   **d.** Finding a job.

Notes restrict：制限する、限定する   imply：ほのめかす

More Word Chunks

1 Underline the word which does NOT collocate with the word in bold. You can use your dictionary.

a.	**get:**	funny	married	home
b.	**have:**	a big heart	a talent	an intelligence
c.	**look:**	around	through	by
d.	**take:**	a favor	me by surprise	your time

Here are some other word chunks made from "get", "have", and "take."

get:	upset	angry
have:	a good sense of humor	something in common with each other
take:	a nap	care of each other

2 Complete the sentences using any of the word chunks from question 1.

a. Sometimes couples who **have nothing** _____ have surprisingly good relationships.

b. Some die-hard sports fans **get** _____ if their team loses, but they don't stay depressed for long.

c. When choosing a career, it is important that you **take** _____ to think about your interests and learn about careers related to those interests.

d. Many people who go on a volunteer vacation **have a** _____ and enjoy helping others.

e. Billy Mills **had** _____ for running.

f. Some MySpace members can spend hours **looking** _____ the personal profiles available on the website.

Notes die-hard：頑固な   stay depressed：落ちこんだままでいる

OUTPUT! Writing

Below is the Clara's personal profile from a social networking site. Work with your partner to put the sentences (a-e) in the correct order so that the profile makes sense.

Clara's Profile

Interests:
- Spending time with family and friends.
- Traveling all over the world.
- Getting good grades in my university classes.

Hi, my name is Clara. After I got a degree in business from my college, I got an office job working behind a desk.

( ) a. I wanted a job that allowed me to do what I loved, which is traveling.

( ) b. Once I graduate with the degree, I hope to get a job that's much better than my old one.

( ) c. It was OK but after a few years I wanted to do something different.

( ) d. I am now studying at a university to get a degree in tourism.

( ) e. The only way to do this was to go back to school to study for the job.

If you have some recommendations for countries to visit, let me know.

Notes degree：学位   recommendation：おすすめ

7 Finding Love

Warm Up

1 What is the best way for these people to find love?

© joyfull / Shutterstock.com

2 What is the best way for you to find love? Rank the different ways below, from 1 (the best for you) to 6 (the worst way for you).

- **a.** _____ At a dance club.
- **b.** _____ Through friends.
- **c.** _____ On the Internet.
- **d.** _____ Through a dating agency.
- **e.** _____ At work/school.
- **f.** _____ Through family.

Notes agency：仲介（業）、代理店

Reading Strategy: Making judgments

When you **judge** something, you decide if it is good or bad, right or wrong, interesting or boring, fair or unfair, strange or normal, etc. For example,

"When I was sixteen, I wanted to date a girl in my class because she had beautiful eyes and a cute nose. I didn't know anything else about her, but I thought I was in love with her."

Do you think the writer's reasons for falling in love with the girl were good reasons or bad reasons?

It is not important how you judge, but it is important that you judge what you read. You can base your judgments on your own knowledge, your personal experience, as well as your opinions and reasoning. At school or college you need to make **judgments** all the time, whenever you write an essay, hold a discussion, or attend a lecture.

Notes judgment：判断   reasoning：推論

Strategy in Focus

1 Read the headline of this news story and look at the picture below. Decide if you agree [✓] or disagree [✗] with these judgments.

a. _____ The woman is too old to get married.

b. _____ This must be true love.

c. _____ The man doesn't love the woman.

2 Now read the news story. Decide if you agree [✓] or disagree [✗] with these judgments.

a. _____ Muhamad and Wook will be very happy together.

b. _____ Being married 21 times is not normal.

c. _____ There must be another reason for Muhamad to marry Wook.

d. _____ This story is not interesting enough to be published in a newspaper.

33-Year-Old Marries 104-Year-Old

In Malaysia, a 33-year-old man married a 104-year-old woman, saying their respect for each other and friendship turned to love.

Local newspapers reported it was Muhamad Noor Che Musa's first marriage and his wife's 21st. According to The Star newspaper, Muhamad said, "I am not after her money, as she is poor. Her only asset is her deep religious knowledge. Through her I can deepen my knowledge of religion."

He also said that many people did not understand his decision to marry Wook Kundor. Some people have said their marriage is strange and have questioned his reasons for marrying a woman 71 years older than himself. However, Muhamad says that he has found peace and happiness since marrying Wook.

Feedback:

Here are some possible judgments for activity 2. Your ideas may be different.

a. The marriage will be difficult because of the age difference.

b. Marrying 21 times is not normal. People may think there is something strange or suspicious about Wook.

c. When there is a big age difference, few people will believe the couple is in love. People may think Muhamad is marrying for money, and Wook is marrying because she is lonely.

d. Marrying 21 times and marrying someone so much older / younger is a story that would interest many people.

Notes turn to ~：～に変わる　be after ~：～のあとを追う　asset [ǽset]：財産　religious：宗教の　deepen：深くする　suspicious：怪しい、疑い深い

Reading A Nightclub Romance

▶▶ Before Reading

❶ Take one minute to scan the text to find the answers.

    a. What are the names of the writer's parents?   _____

    b. Where did the writer's parents meet?   _____

    c. How did the writer's parents meet?   _____

❷ How do you think the writer feels about the way her parents met?

    a. embarrassed   b. happy   c. upset   d. sad   e. ashamed

▶▶ While Reading

❸ As you are reading the text, decide if the writer's mother and father were good friends to Peter.

▶▶ After Reading

❹ Tell a partner your ideas from activity 3 above.

❺ Decide if you agree [✓] or disagree [✗] with these judgments. Then compare your judgments with your partner.

    a. _____ It was wrong of Martha to date someone she wasn't really interested in.

    b. _____ It was OK for Archie to sing a love song to his friend's date.

    c. _____ It was good that Martha paid attention to Peter the rest of the night.

    d. _____ It was good that Martha called Peter to ask for Archie's number.

❻ Match the first part of the sentence to the second part.

    a. At the beginning of the story,   i. was the one.
    b. Martha didn't think that Peter   ii. Archie's phone number.
    c. Peter's friend was singing   iii. Martha was dating Peter.
    d. Archie dedicated a song   iv. at a nightclub.
    e. Martha asked Peter for   v. to the writer's mom.

A Nightclub Romance

[1] Before my mom, Martha, met my dad, she dated a guy named Peter. She knew that Peter wasn't "the one"—the man she wanted to marry—but she enjoyed his company and they had fun hanging out with each other. One day Peter asked Martha if she wanted to go to Ziggy's, a nightclub where a friend of his was singing. She thought that would be fun and agreed to go.

[2] When they arrived at the nightclub, Peter found his friend, Archie, and introduced him to my mom. In an instant, Martha was taken by the tall, attractive guy. He reminded her of Tony Bennett, a famous singer in the 1950s and 60s, whom she really liked. They all chatted for a while and then it was Archie's time to sing.

[3] Martha expected Archie to begin by introducing himself and then singing some of his songs. She couldn't believe it when he opened his act with, "I'd like to dedicate this song to that beautiful woman sitting over there," and he pointed at Martha. The song he sang was the love song, "If I loved you." Martha didn't know what to do. This attractive, talented man was singing to her, right in front of his friend. She glanced at Peter who looked upset and jealous.

[4] Martha decided that the right thing to do was ignore Archie and pay attention to Peter for the rest of the night. After Archie finished, she and Peter left the club to go out to dinner. Peter didn't talk about what had happened and she decided not to mention it.

[5] However, over the next few days, Martha couldn't stop thinking about Archie. She knew she wanted to see him again but she didn't know his phone number or where he was singing next. The only way to find him was to ask Peter. Eventually, she called Peter up and asked for Archie's number—which I'm glad she did, or I wouldn't be telling this story today!

(331 words)

Notes guy：（若い）男性　in an instant：すぐに、即座に　attractive：魅力的な　remind A of B：AにBを思い出させる　chat：おしゃべりする　dedicate：捧げる　glance at ~：~をちらりと見る　jealous：嫉妬している　ignore：無視する、見ない［聞かない］ふりをする

Word Work

❼ Use these word chunks to complete the sentences.

| right in front of | couldn't stop thinking about |
| couldn't believe it | the right thing to do |

a. Martha _____ when Archie started singing to her.

b. Martha was amazed that Archie would sing a love song to her _____ his friend, Peter.

c. She thought that _____ was to pay attention to Peter.

d. At the end of the story, Martha decided to call Archie because she _____ him.

OUTPUT! Speaking

Make a pair. Do these reading aloud activities using the final paragraph of the reading:

a. Listen & Repeat (Chunk)

Student A reads each chunk (below) aloud to Student B, and Student B repeats the chunk without looking at the textbook. Take turns.

> However, / over the next few days, / Martha couldn't stop thinking about Archie. / She knew / she wanted to see him again / but she didn't know / his phone number / or where he was singing next. / The only way to find him / was to ask Peter. / Eventually, / she called Peter up / and asked for Archie's number / — which I'm glad she did, / or I wouldn't be telling this story today!

b. Listen & Repeat (Sentence)

Student A reads each sentence aloud to Student B, and Student B repeats the sentence without looking at the textbook. Take turns.

c. Shadowing

Student A reads the paragraph aloud to Student B while Student B repeats what Student A says as quickly as possible without looking at the textbook. Take turns.

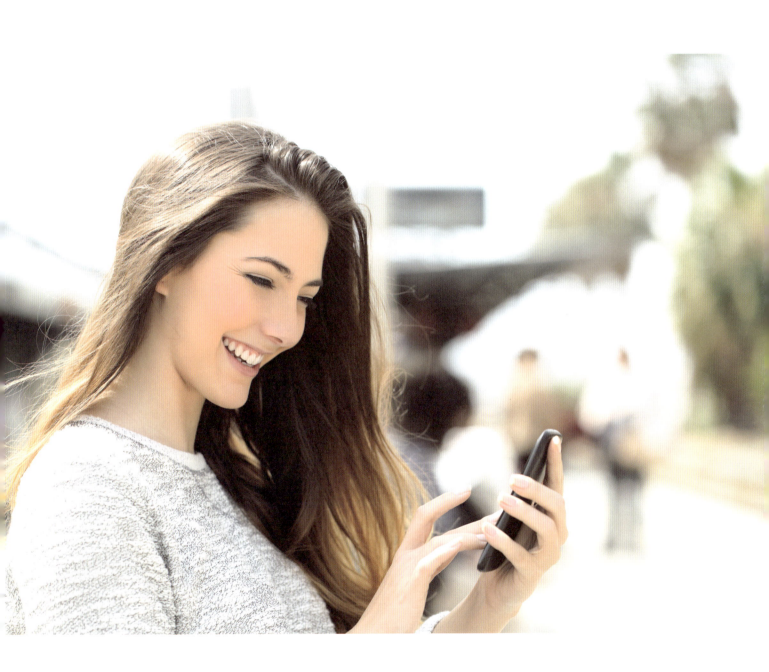

8 Kindness

Warm Up

1 Which of these acts of kindness have you done in the last four weeks?

a. Phoned someone you haven't spoken to in a long time to say "hello".
b. Smiled and said "hello" to someone you don't know.
c. Picked up litter.
d. Opened a door for someone.
e. Visited an elderly neighbor who has no family nearby.
f. Offered to carry someone's heavy shopping bags.
g. Offered to babysit for free.
h. Volunteered to help younger students study at a school.
i. Donated blood.
j. Complimented someone.

2 What was the most generous act of kindness you have done? Write it down.

_____

Notes litter：くず、ごみ donate：寄付する compliment：ほめる generous：寛大な

Reading Strategy: Making associations

While reading, good readers think about similar situations from **their own lives** and **associate** the text with their own personal knowledge.

For example, when reading the sentence, "It was the night before Lisa's final English exam, she was tired and drinking a lot of coffee," readers may think about a similar experience they had. They may think about:

- Where they were studying for their English exam.
- Why they were still studying late.
- How they felt while they were studying.

Readers may also think about their personal knowledge of things connected to the text:

- examinations, such as TOEIC® and TOEFL®.
- the effects of drinking coffee.
- the benefits of studying the night before an examination.

Connecting the text to your experiences and **making associations** can help you understand a situation described in the text more fully.

Notes association：連想 effect：効果、影響 benefit：利益、利点

Strategy in Focus

As you are reading the story *Cold Hands, Warm Heart*, ask yourself the following questions about the text.

Cold Hands, Warm Heart

It was a very cold winter, and I was outside running some errands for my mother.
- a. How cold is the winter in your hometown?
- b. What errands do you run for your family or friends?
- c. Do you prefer to be indoors or outside in the winter?

On the way back to our warm apartment, I saw an old homeless woman. She was dressed in a thin jacket and was begging for spare change.
- d. Are there homeless people in your country?
- e. Where do they stay? How do they get food?

I was a student and broke so I had no money to give her. Yet this old woman was blue with cold and I felt bad not giving her anything. I realized that there was something I could do to help her.
- f. Have you ever been in a situation where you had no money?
- g. When was the last time you were blue with cold?
- h. Have you ever given homeless people money?

I went over to her, pulled off my warm gloves and put them on her hands. I said that I was sorry for not giving any money and that I hoped the gloves would help. The old woman smiled and quietly thanked me.
- i. What did you do the last time you saw a homeless person?
- j. Have you heard or read about any stories about homeless people?

Feedback:
The text is about a student helping a homeless woman. The questions should make you think about similar situations that you have experienced and what you know about homeless people.

Notes run errands for ～：～の使い走りをする　　thin：薄い　　spare change：余分な小銭　　broke：［形］無一文の、お金がない　　pull off ～：（手袋、ブーツなど）～を引っぱって取る、脱ぐ

Reading My Best Friend Dan

▶▶ Before Reading

❶ Read the beginning of the text below, and predict what will happen next.

Walking home from school one day, I saw Dan, a kid from my school, on the other side of the road. I said to myself, "He must be a real nerd." as he was carrying a lot of books. …

   a. Dan was bullied by a group of kids.
   b. Dan was run over by a truck.
   c. Dan sat down and began reading his books.

▶▶ While Reading

❷ Read the first paragraph on the next page and check your answer.

❸ As you read the story, number the pictures in order from 1 to 4.

A _____   B _____   C _____   D _____

▶▶ After Reading

❹ Ask a partner these questions about the text.

Did the story:

   a. make you feel sad/happy …?
   b. have a surprise ending/an unexpected ending …?
   c. have a negative ending/positive ending …?

❺ Choose the correct ending to complete the statements.

   a. At the beginning of the story, Dan •   • i. best friends.
   b. The writer helped Dan •   • ii. thanked the writer for being his friend.
   c. The writer and Dan lived •   • iii. because he felt sorry for him.
   d. The writer and Dan became •   • iv. didn't know the writer.
   e. During high school, Dan •   • v. near each other.
   f. In his speech, Dan •   • vi. became popular.

▶ My Best Friend Dan

[1] Walking home from school one day, I saw Dan, a kid from my school, on the other side of the road. I said to myself, "He must be a real nerd." as he was carrying a lot of books. As I continued walking, I saw a group of kids run into Dan, knocking his books out of his arms and pushing him so he fell over. So, I ran over to help him, and as we were picking up his books, I saw tears in his eyes.

[2] As I helped him stand up, I said, "Those kids are stupid." He looked at me and said, "Thanks." There was a grateful smile on his face.

[3] We started talking and soon realized that we lived near each other. We talked all the way home. Dan turned out to be a pretty cool kid. We hung out all weekend and the more I got to know Dan, the more I liked him. Dan and I became best friends.

[4] Over the next four years, he became more popular and all the girls loved him. In our senior year, Dan got the best grades in our class, and had to give a speech for graduation.

[5] As Dan started his speech, he looked at me. "Graduation is a time to thank the people who helped you survive those tough years—your parents, your teachers, but mostly your friends. Being a friend is the best gift you can give. I'm going to tell you a story." I just looked at Dan in amazement as he told the story of the first day we met. He had planned to drop out of school and run away from home that weekend. Dan talked of how he had emptied his locker so his mom wouldn't have to do it later and was carrying all of his books home. He looked hard at me and gave me a little smile. "Thankfully, I was saved. My friend saved me from making a huge mistake." Everyone looked at Dan in shock as he told us about his weakest moment.

(346 words)

Notes nerd：頭は良いが社会性がない人、何かにのめりこんでいる人、おたく　run into ~：~にぶつかる、衝突する　knock A B：Aを打って［に当たって］Bの状態にする　tear：涙　grateful：感謝した、謝意を表す　turn out to ...：…であることがわかる　senior：大学4年生（1年生は freshman、2年生は sophomore、3年生は junior と呼ばれる）　grade：成績　survive：生き残る、（逆境に）耐える　drop out of ~：退学する、逃避する　empty：［動］（入れ物）をからにする　so S V ...：(= so that S V ...) SがV…するように

▍Word Work

❻ Complete the sentences with a word chunk from the text.

| run away from home | dropped out of school | hung out | all the way |

a. My friend Sarah never studied and wasn't interested in going to college. She _____ at 16 and got a job in a fast food restaurant. She now wishes she had stayed in school.

b. I couldn't afford to fly to California for a job interview, so I drove _____ from New York. It took five days to get there.

c. Many teenagers find their lives very stressful and sometimes want to _____.

d. I had a great time this weekend. I _____ with my best friend the whole time.

OUTPUT! Writing & Speaking

The author of the story did something that helped Dan change his life. But what **would have happened** if the author **had NOT helped** Dan? Write your stories. When finished, share your ideas with your partner.

(Example) After knocked to the ground, Dan **would have** <u>run away from the group of kids without picking up his books</u>.

a. When getting back home, Dan **would have** _____

b. After running away from home, Dan **would have** _____

c. After Dan's running away from home, his parents _____

d. In his new place, Dan _____

9 Bravery

Warm Up

Look at the pictures and rank them from 1 (bravest) to 6 (least brave).

A _____

B _____

C _____

D _____

E _____

F _____

Reading Strategy: Deducing the meaning of words from context

You can find words you don't understand when reading in your first language as well as your second language. However, you can't always use a dictionary to understand every word in a text. Often it is better to guess the meaning of words from the context—or situation—you find them in. This is called **deducing** (or guessing) **meaning from context**.

For example, what does the word "valiantly" mean in the sentence below?

"The brave firefighters tried valiantly to save the family's pet from the burning house."

   a. quietly
   b. bravely
   c. slowly

You would probably choose bravely, because firefighters are trying to save a pet in a house that is burning. The correct answer must be b. as the firefighters are acting bravely.

Notes　deduce：推論する

Strategy in Focus

1 Look at the picture. What do you think "toxic" means?

a. Very tasty.
b. Very dangerous.
c. Very spicy.

Feedback:
The correct answer is b. You should be able to guess that toxic means very dangerous because the label is telling you not to drink the liquid and has a symbol warning of danger.

2 Look at the picture. What do you think "flammable" means?

a. Cannot catch fire easily.
b. Can catch fire easily.
c. Can get dirty easily.

Feedback:
The correct answer is b. You should be able to guess that flammable means "can catch fire easily" because the label is telling you not to leave it near heat and has a symbol warning of fire.

3 Guess the meaning of the bold words in these sentences.

a. The birds are **soaring** above the clouds. They look like small airplanes.

    i. making a noise   ii. flying high   iii. feeling scared

b. Sam Jones received a medal of **valor** from the mayor for running into a burning building and saving the lives of two children.

    i. bravery   ii. cowardice   iii. weakness.

c. Jane makes friends wherever she goes because of her **gregarious** personality.

    i. outgoing   ii. shy   iii. aggressive

Feedback:

a. The correct answer is ii. The sentence is about birds, and birds fly. Also, soaring is a verb and the birds are doing this above the clouds, so they must be flying high.

b. The correct answer is i. Someone who risks his or her life to run into a burning building is brave. A medal of valor recognizes an act of bravery.

c. The correct answer is i. People like Jane and she makes friends easily.

Notes liquid：[líkwid] 液体 warning：警告 extremely：極度に、たいへん scared：おびえた、おそれている cowardice：[káuərdis] おくびょう

Reading: A True Hero • 63

Reading A True Hero

▶▶ **Before Reading**

❶ Look at the pictures below and guess what the story is about.

  a. Three people who save other people's lives.
  b. A father who tests his three sons.
  c. The ways people can help others.

▶▶ **While Reading**

❷ Read the first and second paragraphs and check your hypothesis.

❸ Read the rest of the story and put the pictures in order.

A _____ B _____ C _____ D _____

▶▶ **After Reading**

❹ Ask a partner these questions about the text.

  a. Do you think the father made the right decision?
  b. Who do you think is the most generous person? Why?

❺ Find these words in the story and work out their meaning.

  a. gathered (line 15)
   i. met
   ii. talked
  b. drowning (line 25)
   i. die under water
   ii. die from falling from a high building
  c. on the edge (line 35)
   i. close to the end of the cliff
   ii. far from the end of the cliff
  d. enemy (line 40)
   i. friend
   ii. opponent
  e. dragged (line 42)
   i. moved easily
   ii. moved with difficulty
  f. swore (line 45)
   i. promised
   ii. spoke impolitely

A True Hero

[1] There once was a poor father who lived with his three sons. The father was very old and knew that he would die soon. The only thing he owned of value was a diamond, but he couldn't decide who to give it to because he loved all his sons the same.

[2] One day, he called his sons to his bedroom and said, "Sons, as you know, the only valuable thing I have is a diamond. I do not want to sell it, but I cannot choose who to give it to. So, I have decided to give the diamond to the son who does the greatest good. Return in one week and tell me what good things you have done."

[3] After a week, the sons all gathered together again at the father's bed. "Oldest son, tell me what good deed you did," the old man said.

[4] The oldest son told his father that he had given half of everything he owned to the poor people in their city. The father thought this was good but not good enough because everyone should help the poor.

[5] The second son told him how he saved a little girl who was drowning in the river. Although the son wasn't a good swimmer, he had risked his own life to save the child. The father thought this was better but everyone should do what they can to save a child.

[6] "Now, what have you done, my youngest child?" the old man asked.

[7] The third son began to tell his story. One day while walking, he saw a man sleeping on the edge of a cliff. If the man rolled the wrong way, he would fall over the cliff. The son decided to go to the man and move him away from the cliff. When he got closer, he realized that the man was Sancho, his enemy, a man who had promised to kill him. Yet, the youngest son decided to help him and dragged him away from the cliff. When Sancho awoke, he couldn't believe that he had been saved and the two men swore to be friends.

[8] The father was very proud of this last act. "You are truly kind. Few people would do something to save their enemy. I will give you the diamond."

(381 words)

Notes　of value：価値がある（= valuable）　good：[名] 善、善いおこない　deed：行為、おこない　cliff：がけ、絶壁　awoke：(awake「目覚める」の過去形)

Word Work

6 Use three of these word chunks from the story to write sentences about yourself, your family or your friends.

| elderly father | gathered together | a poor man | the youngest child |
| is proud of | risked his own life | tell his story | on the edge of |

a. _____

b. _____

c. _____

OUTPUT! Speaking

Look at the pictures in While Reading **3**. Describe the pictures in order and tell the story to your partner. You cannot look at the reading passage.

Review 3

Review of Reading Strategies

- Unit 7: Making judgments
- Unit 8: Making associations
- Unit 9: Deducing the meaning of words from context

1 Which reading strategies do these sentences describe? Read each statement and check [✓] the best answer.

	Making Judgments	Making Associations	Deducing Meaning
a. Think about something that happened in your own life that is similar to something in the text.			
b. Decide if a person in the text is good or bad.			
c. Think about the situation in the text to understand new words.			
d. Decide if you agree or disagree with an opinion in the text.			
e. Think about the context in the text to guess the meaning of the words you don't know.			
f. Think about something you know that is connected to the text.			

2 Read the text and decide if you agree [✓] or disagree [✗] with these judgments. Then compare your judgments with a partner.

a. _____ Surfing in the sea is more dangerous than I thought it was.

b. _____ It is not good for people to surf in the sea.

c. _____ It is very good that Bethany tells her story to inspire others.

3 Write a check [✓] if you thought about these things when you read the text or a cross [✗] if you didn't. Tell a partner what you thought about.

a. _____ scenery of Hawaii   b. _____ walking on the beach

c. _____ surfing in the ocean   d. _____ sight of bleeding

e. _____ JAWS   f. _____ lying on the hospital bed

4 Match the words from the text with their synonyms. Deduce the meaning of each word from its context in the text.

a. attack   •   •   i. having a physical challenge

b. apply   •   •   ii. put on

c. head to   •   •   iii. hurt

d. disabled   •   •   iv. go to

Notes synonym：同義［意］語

Reading ▶ Riding the Wave

[1] Bethany Hamilton, a 13-year-old champion surfer, was in the water waiting for the next wave. It was a beautiful morning in Hawaii and she was surfing with her best friend, Alana, and her friend's father. Bethany was lying on her surfboard with her left arm hanging in the water when she felt something grab it. Suddenly she saw the blood and realized a shark had attacked her.

[2] The shark swam off with Bethany's arm while Bethany called to the others that she needed to get back to shore—a 15-minute swim. Alana's father quickly came over, applied a tourniquet to stop the bleeding, and the group headed to the beach. Luckily, Bethany made it to the hospital in time to save her life.

[3] Most people would probably stop surfing after a shark attack, but Bethany was determined to continue. Ten weeks after the attack, she competed in a surfing event and placed fifth. She has since entered numerous competitions and has even placed first in a few of them.

[4] Bethany only goes into the water when sharks are not feeding, but she still sees sharks. How does she remain calm? Singing and trying to focus on having fun and surfing. Although Bethany is busy with school and surfing, she makes time to help raise money for disabled children around the world. For her courage and positive attitude, Bethany has received numerous awards and she uses her story to inspire others to overcome adversity.

(247 words)

Notes grab:（不意に）つかむ　shore:海岸　bleeding:出血　make it to ~:〜にたどり着く、間に合う　compete:競う、張り合う　feed:［動物が］物を食う、捕食する　raise:上げる、（お金を）集める　courage:勇気　attitude:姿勢、態度　award:賞、賞金　inspire:引き起こす、（人を鼓舞して、促して）〜させる、生気（希望）を与える

Comprehension Check

1 The word "tourniquet" in paragraph 2 is closest in meaning to:
   a. surf board   b. bandage   c. bathing suit   d. sunglasses

2 The word "numerous" in paragraph 3 is closest in meaning to:
   a. one   b. some   c. few   d. many

3 The word "adversity" in paragraph 4 is closest in meaning to:
   a. problem   b. sharks   c. advertisement   d. advantage

4 Decide if the statements are true (T) or false (F).
   a. T F Bethany Hamilton was a very good surfer before the shark attack.
   b. T F Bethany was close to the beach when she was attacked.
   c. T F Bethany's friend was also attacked.
   d. T F It took Bethany ten months to recover from the attack.
   e. T F Bethany's career as a surfer is over.
   f. T F Bethany only surfs where there are no sharks.
   g. T F Bethany gives a lot of inspiring speeches using her experiences.

Notes   bantage：包帯   bathing suit：水着

More Word Chunks

1 Correct the mistakes in the bold word chunks.
   a. Archie sang a love song to Martha **before in front of** his friend, Peter.
   b. Martha thought that **the true thing to do** is to ignore Archie.
   c. Martha decided to call Archie because she **couldn't stop think about** him.
   d. Dan said he had planned to **drop away of** school when he was in high school.
   e. Dan and I talked **every the way** from school back home.
   f. The father **was pride of** his youngest son.
   g. The son began to **speak his story**.
   h. She **made it to the hospital at time** to **rescue her life**.
   i. Bethany **does time** to help **build money** for **poor**.

2 Complete the sentences using any of the word chunks in question 1.
   a. The students need to _____ for their trip.
   b. I only had ten minutes to get to my interview, and I thought I would be late. Luckily, I was able to get a taxi and I _____.

c. I was surprised to know that Steve Jobs, the founder of the world-famous Apple Computer Inc., had _____ college when he was young.

d. My father is a very busy international businessman. Last week on Monday, he left home to take a business trip _____ to Spain, then to Canada and Mexico, and came back in Japan on Thursday.

e. My best friend was a life guard working on the beach in Florida last summer. On her last day at work she heard a man shouting for help. My friend swam out into the ocean and brought the man back to shore. Apparently, the man was very rich and bought my friend a car because she _____.

f. She has three children, all of whom are well-behaved and get good grades at school. She may well _____ them.

g. The cat suddenly came out _____ the bus and was run over.

h. Ana was so desperate to see her fiancé, Ken, that she _____ him.

Notes founder：創立者、設立者 Apple Computer Inc.：アップル・コンピュータ（IT 企業） apparently：実際のところ well-behaved：態度がよい may well：…するのももっともだ run over：（車で）ひく

OUTPUT! Speaking

Ask a partner these questions about the text.

1) Do you think Bethany Hamilton is brave or crazy to continue surfing? Why?
2) Would you continue surfing after a shark attack? Why?

Reading: Riding the Wave

10 Urban Legends

Warm Up

1 What is an "urban legend"? Read the text below and write the Japanese meaning.

An "urban legend" is like a modern folktale. It may be true, but usually it isn't true or we cannot confirm if the story is true. Urban legends are often sent by email as something that happened to a "friend of a friend."

urban legend: _____

2 Look at the three urban legends. One is true and two are false. Which urban legend do you think is true?

a. Using a cell phone at the gas station can cause explosions.

b. There is a woman with her mouth torn to her ears.

c. A woman tried to dry her wet cat in her microwave oven.

Notes　modern：現代の　folktale：民話　confirm：確認する　torn：(tear「引き裂く」の過去分詞形)

Reading Strategy: Visualizing

Most people see pictures (images) in their mind while reading. This is called **visualization**.

Readers will often see images of actions, people, and places. For example, when reading a newspaper article about education, readers may see their old school, teachers, and classrooms.

Visualizing helps the reader understand the text and remember it more effectively. **Visualizing** also helps you deduce the meaning of words from context more easily, as well as helping you to make inferences, interpretations, and judgments.

Notes　visualize：（イメージを）視覚化する、心に思い浮かべる

Strategy in Focus

1 Read the story carefully, and decide what you think about this urban legend.

    a. It is true.   **b.** It never happened.   **c.** It is possible.   **d.** It is impossible.

A Class Psychology Experiment

A class of psychology students decided to carry out an experiment on their professor. They paid attention to the professor's lectures only when he was standing near a waste paper basket. Whenever the professor walked away from the waste paper basket, the students stopped listening to him and started talking. Eventually the professor was "trained" to stand next to the waste paper basket for the whole lecture.

The students then started turning the waste paper basket upside-down before every class. They trained the professor to lecture first with one foot on the waste paper basket, and then stand with both feet on the wastebasket. The experiment worked so well that the professor eventually began giving his lectures while standing on the waste paper basket.

2 Circle the images you visualized in your mind while reading the story.

    a professor   students   a waste paper basket   a classroom

    students listening   students talking   a student moving the wastebasket

    a professor standing on a wastepaper basket

Feedback:

While reading this urban legend, it is common to see the professor and the students in the classroom. You may have seen images from your own life, when you were younger or now. You may also have remembered the smells and noises from classrooms you are familiar with.

Notes experiment：実験　waste：[wéist] くず、ごみ　train：[動] 訓練する、(〜するよう) 仕こむ

Reading The Hairy Hitchhiker

▶▶ Before Reading

❶ Look at the pictures below. Tell a partner who you would help if you saw them hitchhiking and why.

❷ Read the first two sentences of the story below. What do you think the story will be about?

A young woman was driving back home from a party late one rainy night. She had been driving for 20 minutes on a country road when she saw a gray-haired woman by the side of the road.

   a. ____ Tips for hitchhiking.
   b. ____ Why people should not give rides to strangers.
   c. ____ A scary story about an old woman.

▶▶ While Reading

❸ As you read the story, try to visualize images in your mind, and decide if this urban legend is true.

▶▶ After Reading

❹ Check [✓] any of these images you visualized in your mind while reading the story. Describe these images and any other images you visualized to a partner.

   a. ____ A young woman driving on a small dark road.
   b. ____ An old woman talking to the driver through an open window.
   c. ____ The old woman sitting in the back of a dark car.
   d. ____ A hairy arm with a tattoo.

❺ What do you think of this urban legend?

   a. It is true. This could happen.
   b. It is not true. I don't believe this happened.
   c. I have heard this story before, so it could be true.
   d. I have heard this story before, but it is not true.

The Hairy Hitchhiker

[1] A young woman was driving back home from a party late one rainy night. She had been driving for 20 minutes on a country road when she saw a gray-haired woman by the side of the road. Usually, Mary never picked up hitchhikers, but it was a cold night and it was an old woman, so she stopped her car. Mary asked the old woman if she needed a ride. The old woman nodded and got in.

[2] "Do you live near here?" Mary asked.

[3] "No," answered the passenger, in a soft voice, "I'm just going to visit a friend. He was going to meet me, but his car won't start, so I decided to hitchhike. There isn't a bus at this time, but I knew someone would give me a ride."

[4] Something in the way the old lady spoke made Mary uneasy about this strange hitchhiker. She didn't know why, but Mary felt that there was something wrong, something dangerous. But how could an old lady be dangerous?

[5] The hitchhiker turned to give the young driver some candy. As she took the candy, Mary noticed the old woman's hands were very large, and had no wrinkles. She also saw thick hair and a tattoo on the woman's left arm. This wasn't an old woman. It was a young man!

[6] Mary was scared and didn't know what to do, but she quickly thought of a plan. She suddenly stopped the car and said she had hit something. She asked the old woman to take a look. When the hitchhiker was out of the car, Mary drove off.

[7] Thinking she had made a mistake, Mary felt guilty—the hitchhiker was surely not a young man meaning she had left an old woman at the side of a road far from any houses. She felt even worse when she noticed she still had the old woman's bag in her car. She opened the bag to look for information about the hitchhiker's identity and saw that it was filled with wallets, jewelry, and a large, bloody knife.

(343 words)

Notes hairy：毛深い　pick up：（人を）車に乗せる　passenger：乗客　give ~ a ride：~を車に乗せる（= give a ride to ~）　wrinkle：しわ　thick：（髪などが）濃い、厚みのある　guilty：やましい、罪の意識がある　identity：身元

Word Work

6 Rewrite the word chunks to correct the mistakes according to the story.

a. A young woman was **driving return home** from a party late one rainy night.
_____

b. She asked the old woman if she **needed a drop off**.
_____

c. The young woman was scared and **didn't know what to make**.
_____

d. She asked the old lady to **take a watch**.
_____

e. The young woman immediately **thought guilty**.
_____

OUTPUT! Writing & Speaking

Look at the pictures below. With a partner, create a story in English. When finished, tell it to the class.

Notes

hail a taxi：タクシーを呼びとめる
rear seat：後部座席
after a while：しばらくして
disappear：消える、いなくなる
get wet：（水で）濡れる

Reading: The Hairy Hitchhiker • 77

11 Relationship Myths

Warm Up

1 What is the relationship between the people in the pictures (e.g., friends, work colleagues etc.)? Write your idea under each picture.

A _____

B _____

C _____

> **Notes**　myth：神話、作り話　colleague：同僚

Reading Strategy: Summarizing

While and after reading a text, it is often useful to **summarize** what you have read. You can do this in your mind, and you can also write a **summary**.

When you summarize a text, you identify the main ideas and other important information, but do not have to give too many details.

These questions will help you summarize a text:

- What (Who) is the text about?
- What happens? When? Where?
- Why did the author write the text?

Now read the following news story and choose the best summary:

> James Blake knew something was wrong when he walked into the bank. Blake, the bank manager of New York Trust, noticed that the overnight security guard was missing. He then saw that the doors to the bank vault were open. When Blake went into the vault, he noticed that all the money was missing. Blake's bank was one of three banks in the city that was robbed last night.

a. There were three bank robberies in New York last night. The New York Trust was one of them.
b. James Blake, the bank manager of New York Trust, was very surprised that his bank was robbed. He noticed that the security guard and money were missing.
c. New York Trust was robbed last night. It was the third time this bank was robbed.

Feedback:
The best summary is a. as it provides the key ideas in the text. Answer b. gives too many details and c. is inaccurate.

> **Notes**　summarize：要約する　detail：詳細　bank vault：銀行の金庫室　rob：盗む　robbery：強盗　inaccurate：不正確な

Strategy in Focus

1 As you read the article, underline the most important ideas.

Happily Ever After?

Sally Gregory is putting her seven-year-old daughter to bed. Gregory's daughter is begging for her mom to read her the fairy tale, *Cinderella*. Although Gregory loves reading to her child, she does not like the message contained in the popular fairy tale.

"This fairy tale portrays the stepmother as evil, stepsisters as cheats and liars, and a girl who is passively waiting for her prince to come. I don't want my daughter to think that she has to wait for one true love to find her. I want her to question all the messages contained in such stories." Gregory says.

She isn't the only person to feel this way. A group of like-minded people started the group, Fairy Tale Busters. Their aim is to "bust", or show the truth, in fairy tales like *Cinderella* and *Snow White*. Just like Gregory, they want parents and children to challenge the messages contained in these stories.

2 Now read the summaries and decide which one is the best.

a. The article *Happily Ever After?* is about children getting false ideas about relationships from fairy tales. The group, "Fairy Tale Busters," wants children to question the messages contained in these popular stories.

b. The article discusses the lessons children can learn from reading popular fairy tales. Sally Gregory believes girls should be passive and wait for their "prince" to rescue them from their problems.

c. Sally Gregory doesn't want to read *Cinderella* to her daughter. It is her daughter's favorite story but it contains negative messages about stepmothers and sisters. Other parents don't like this fairy tale so they have started a group called "Fairy Tale Busters." The group wants to show the world that the messages behind *Cinderella* and *Snow White* are negative.

Feedback:

The best summary is a. The main idea of the reading is that children learn unrealistic messages from fairy tales.

Summary b. is not a good summary because some of the information is not correct. The writer does not want girls to wait for their prince.

Summary c. is not a good summary because it contains too many unimportant details.

Notes ever after：その後ずっと　fairy tale：おとぎ話　portray：描く　evil：悪、邪悪　cheat：［名］詐欺師　liar：うそつき　passively：受動的に、消極的に　like-minded：同じ考え方［意見、趣味］を持っている　aim：目的　bust：こわす

Reading Dating Myths

▶▶ **Before Reading**

❶ Decide if you agree [✓] or disagree [✗] with these statements. Then discuss your answers with a partner.

   a. ____ Your boyfriend/girlfriend should be your best friend.
   b. ____ You should never fight with your boyfriend/girlfriend.
   c. ____ You should have the same interests as your partner.
   d. ____ As long as you love each other, money is not important.
   e. ____ If your partner has a bad habit, you can change it.

▶▶ **While Reading**

❷ As you read the text, underline the important ideas. For example, you may want to underline the ideas that tell you:

   • What the text is about.
   • Who the text is about.
   • What the writer thinks.

▶▶ **After Reading**

❸ Choose the best ending to the summary.

The article describes some of the ideas people have about romantic relationships. ...

   a. It explains that couples in long-term relationships will eventually share the same interests and become very good friends. Often these couples become very similar and learn to change to make each other happy.
   b. It explains that many couples say they are perfect for each other because they don't argue and they share the same interests. However, it is natural and healthy to argue if you still respect your partner.
   c. It explains that sometimes it is healthy to argue with your partner, and that you don't have to share all your partner's interests. The article also explains that it is important to keep your friends and not to try to change your partner.

❹ According to the text, are these statements true (T) or false (F)?

   a. T F In a good relationship, a couple doesn't have to agree on everything.
   b. T F In a perfect relationship, you share all the same interests as your partner.
   c. T F It is important to maintain friendships with other people while dating.
   d. T F Asking your partner to change something about himself/herself is OK if it will make you happier.

Dating Myths

[1] Many people have a certain idea about what makes a good relationship. Often it is connected to always getting along, being madly in love, and having the same interests, but many experts say that relying on this idea is actually a recipe for disaster. These are common myths learned from fairy tales and popular movies. A healthy relationship is much more complex than what you see in the movies.

A healthy couple doesn't fight

[2] It is natural to have disagreements with your partner. The important thing is how you deal with your differences. Do you walk away or yell if you don't get your way, or do you listen to what your partner has to say? It is healthy to argue or fight as long as you respect the other person's ideas and feelings.

A good couple should be interested in the same things

[3] Although it is important to share some interests, don't change what you like to do just because your partner doesn't like the same thing. If you try to be something you are not, you may start to resent your partner.

Your partner should be your best friend

[4] Your partner is the person you spend the most time with, but should you be best friends? Maybe not. Don't forget the person who was your best friend before you started dating. Who else can you talk to about any problems you have in your relationship?

I'll be happy once my partner changes

[5] This is one of the biggest relationship myths around. A partner is NOT a project. If you think, "I'd love him more if he were more ...," maybe you need to reconsider your relationship.

(278 words)

Notes a certain ~：ある（ひとつの）～   get along：仲良くする   madly：狂ったように   recipe：（料理の）レシピ、（何かの）原因   disaster：災難   complex：複雑な   deal with ~：～を処理する、～に対処する   get one's way：（自分の）思い通りにする   argue：言い争う、議論する   resent：腹を立てる   project：プロジェクト（ビジネスの企画のように計画・改善していくもの）   reconsider：再考する

Word Work

5 Complete the sentences with these word chunks.

| walked away | don't get my way | deal with our differences | are madly in love |

a. I was so angry after the fight with my boyfriend that I _____.

b. My girlfriend and I _____. When we're not together, we're always talking on the phone.

c. I get angry when my parents don't let me go out dancing or watch late-night TV. I hate it when I _____.

d. My best friend and I _____ in different ways. I like to talk about them but he likes to ignore them and pretend they don't exist.

OUTPUT! Writing

Below is the summary of "A True Hero" you read in Unit 9 (p. 65). Skim the article again, and complete the summary.

The article "A True ( )" is about an old ( ) who was going to ( ) soon. One day he ( ) his three sons that ( ) would give his diamond ( ) the son who does ( ) greatest good. A week ( ), the sons gathered at ( ) father's bed, and told ( ) they did. The oldest ( ) said that he had ( ) the poor by giving ( ) of everything he owned. ( ) second son said he ( ) saved a little girl ( ) in the river. The ( ) thought these were good ( ) not good enough. But ( ) he heard that the ( ) son had saved his ( ), he was proud of ( ) youngest son's act and ( ) to give him the ( ).

12 Adventure

Warm Up

What is the best way to have an adventure? Rank these different adventures from 1 (the best way for you) to 4 (the worst way for you).

© Suvorov_Alex / Shutterstock.com

A

B

C

D

Reading Strategy: Planning your reading

To read effectively, you must understand the task—the reason why you are reading. Are you reading:

- for pleasure and interest?
- to take a multiple choice test?
- to take part in a discussion?
- to write an essay?

It is important to **know why you are reading** something. Then you can plan how carefully you need to read it, and plan how much time you want to spend reading.

For example, if you are going to read a best-selling novel **for pleasure**, you would probably read the whole text quickly and not too carefully.

In a **multiple choice test**, you would read the question first and scan the text looking for key words, facts, names, or dates to give you the answer.

If you are using the text to give you ideas **for a discussion**, you don't need to understand the whole text, so you could skim the text looking for its main ideas. You only need to contribute to the discussion with what you understand and agree with.

When you are preparing **to write an essay**, you usually read a text carefully so you understand its ideas well and how the ideas are supported. You may want to include the ideas in your essay with your own examples, adding your own thoughts.

Notes task：課題、やるべきこと   pleasure：楽しみ   multiple choice：多肢選択の   contribute：貢献する

Strategy in Focus

1 You are reading the following article because you think it may be interesting. Decide how to read the story.

　　a. Scan for key words and facts.　　**b.** Skim for the main ideas.
　　c. Read everything carefully.　　**d.** Read everything one time quickly.

2 Read the story.

Rover's Great Adventure

Rover, a Golden Retriever dog, survived a 160-foot fall down a cliff in southern California yesterday. After tumbling down the cliff, Rover landed next to the busy Pacific Coast Highway and just missed being hit by a truck.

A motorist who was parked nearby and had witnessed the events whistled for Rover, who jumped straight into her car. The rescuer says that as soon as Rover got into the car, he started licking her face.

But Rover's owner did not know about the rescue. Karl Robinson lost sight of Rover when the dog started to chase a wild rabbit. Robinson ran to the cliff and started looking for his dog. Robinson ended up getting stuck himself as he attempted to climb down the cliff to find Rover and he had to call for help using his cell phone.

Robinson was eventually rescued by firefighters and he was quickly reunited with Rover.

3 You are going to answer a multiple choice question about the news story. Decide how you will read the text this time.

　　a. Read everything one time quickly.　　**b.** Read everything carefully.
　　c. Skim for the main ideas.　　**d.** Scan for key words and facts.

4 Answer this multiple choice question about the text.

Robinson is the:

　　a. Name of the dog.　　**b.** The dog's owner.
　　c. The women who rescued the dog.　　**d.** The firefighter who rescued the dog.

Feedback:
The answers are 1 d., 3 d., and 4 b.

Notes foot：フット、フィート（長さの単位：1 foot = 30.48 cm）　tumble down：転げ落ちる　land：［動］着陸する、地面に着く　just missed -ing：もうちょっとで〜するところだった　motorist：（自家用車の）ドライバー　witness：目撃する　whistle：口笛を吹く　lick：なめる　lose sight of 〜：〜を見失う　chase：追いかける　end up –ing：結局…することになる　get stuck：行き詰る　attempt to …：…しようとする、試みる　be reunited with 〜：〜と再会する

Reading: My Australian Adventure • 85

Reading My Australian Adventure

▶▶ Before Reading

❶ Your teacher suggests that you read *My Australian Adventure* because you will be asked to join a discussion and talk about the story. Decide how you will read the article.

    a. _____ Scan for key words and facts.   **b.** _____ Skim for the main ideas.

    c. _____ Read everything carefully.   **d.** _____ Read everything one time quickly.

❷ Make a list of words/things you associate with Australia.

_____   _____   _____   _____

_____   _____   _____   _____

▶▶ While Reading

❸ While you read the story, try to visualize images in your mind.

▶▶ After Reading

❹ Describe the clearest image you visualized to a partner.

❺ Tell your partner if you found the story:

    a. interesting   **b.** amusing   **c.** boring   **d.** silly

❻ Tell your partner about a trip you have taken, answering these questions:

    Where did you go?   When did you go?   How long did you go for?

    Who did you go with?   What did you do?   Did you have a good time?

❼ Read the story again. Check [✓] the inferences you can make.

    a. ____ The conference was in Brisbane.
    b. ____ Chris hit a kangaroo when he was driving too quickly.
    c. ____ Chris thought the kangaroo was dead.
    d. ____ Chris saved the kangaroo's life.
    e. ____ Chris and the writer found the kangaroo, and got the jacket back.
    f. ____ Chris and the writer didn't have extra car keys.

My Australian Adventure

[1] A couple of years ago, I went to Australia for a conference with my colleague, Chris. We decided to drive across country to Brisbane after the conference ended. The drive was going to take four days and most of it was across the desert, so we had to take food, water, and extra gas with us.

[2] The first day was a lot of fun as we were excited and laughing at each other's stupid jokes. By the third day of driving in the seemingly endless desert, we began to get bored. We had been quiet for a few hours when in the distance Chris spotted some kangaroos. We were both excited and decided to get a closer look. Chris accelerated to catch up with the kangaroos. We got closer and closer, and Chris was doing 110 kilometers per hour. We were very close to the kangaroos—too close—when we heard a loud BANG!

[3] Chris stopped the car and we got out. Behind the car was a large kangaroo lying completely still on the ground. Chris went over to the kangaroo and put his baseball cap on its head. He took off his sunglasses and put them on the kangaroo and did the same with his jacket. Then, he put his arm around the kangaroo and told me to take a photo of them together. I was still in shock, but I took out my camera. While I was focusing the camera, I saw the kangaroo move. It suddenly woke up, looked at Chris, and hopped away into the distance before we could do anything.

[4] I started laughing but Chris looked very serious. He said his wallet and passport were in the jacket. I started laughing even harder. I stopped laughing, however, when he said that our car keys were also in the jacket!

(306 words)

Word Work

8 Rewrite the word chunks to correct the mistakes.

a. There was a large crowd gathering on the other side of the street, so I crossed the road to **take a nearer look**. They were watching some young kids dancing.

_____

b. **A few of years ago** I went camping with my friends. We had a great time.

_____

c. I want to go to China one day, so I can **give a photo** standing on the Great Wall.

_____

d. Whenever I am feeling sad, my mom **takes her arm over me** to help me feel better.

_____

OUTPUT! Writing

Below is the summary of the passage "My Australian Adventure." Complete the sentence a-g using the words provided in ( ).

A couple of years ago, the author and his colleague, Chris, took a car trip across Australia.

a. (desert, kangaroos)

_____

_____

b. (closer, kangaroos, hit)

_____

_____

c. (Chris, over, put, jacket)

_____

_____

d. (arm, author, photo)

_____

_____

e. (suddenly, woke, hopped)

_____

_____

f. (laughed, because, lost, wallet and passport, jacket)

_____

_____

g. (author, stopped, when, keys)

_____

_____

Review 4

Review of Reading Strategies

- Unit 10: Visualizing
- Unit 11: Summarizing
- Unit 12: Planning your reading

1 Which reading strategies do these sentences describe? Read each statement and check [✓] the best answer.

	Visualizing	Summarizing	Planning Your Reading
a. Think about the reason why you are reading the text.			
b. Think about who and what the text is about.			
c. See images in your mind of people in the text.			
d. Decide if you are reading the text for pleasure or a test.			
e. See pictures in your mind of places in the text.			
f. Remember the main ideas of the text.			

2 You are going to read a news article to write an essay. Decide how to read the text.

a. _____ Scan for key words and facts.   b. _____ Skim for the main ideas.

c. _____ Read everything carefully.   d. _____ Read everything one time quickly.

3 As you read the text, try to visualize images. After you have read the text, tell a partner about the images you saw.

4 In groups, discuss if corporal punishment in schools should be legal.

5 Choose the best ending to the summary.

In the article, the writer describes her ideas about corporal punishment. ...

a. She says that although many American states allow corporal punishment in schools, it can cause psychological damage to the students, encourage them to be violent as adults, and cause physical harm.

b. She says that 300,000 schools in America discipline students with corporal punishment. They allow teachers to hit, beat and paddle students. She also says that students should be punished each day in these schools.

Notes legal：法律の、合法の

Reading ▶ Corporal Punishment in U.S. Schools

Student : Marta Sanchez
Professor : Linda Lane
Date : August 13, 2008

[1] Parents send their children to school to be educated and learn how to behave in the community. Most parents assume that school is a safe environment yet they may not know that when their children get into trouble they could be physically harmed. Many U.S. schools still use corporal punishment, such as hitting, beating, or paddling for disciplinary purposes.

[2] According to federal statistics, over 300,000 American school children were disciplined with corporal punishment in the year 2002-3, and 22 states still allow it to be used in schools, including Texas and Louisiana. I think that corporal punishment should be stopped. Hitting has physical effects on students and may also cause psychological damage. Adults are responsible for taking care of children, not harming them.

[3] One reason why we should stop corporal punishment in our schools is that this method has harmful psychological effects on children. Many children may lie and not take responsibility for their bad behavior because they are afraid of the punishment. Moreover, punishing children this way can lead to further violence. Studies have found that children who were hit often turned into adults who do not get along with others and used violence against their own loved ones.

[4] When corporal punishment is allowed in schools, it becomes easier for some adults to hurt children. There are many reports of students who have been severely beaten in schools that allow corporal punishment. When parents realize that their own children may be physically harmed, they are often against the idea of using corporal punishment as a method of discipline. Although they want their children to behave in school, they don't want them to be hurt.

[5] The best way of dealing with children's misbehavior is by preventing it. Parents and teachers should work together to encourage children to be responsible and respectful in the classroom. Adults and children should talk openly and deal with their differences in a non-violent way. If punishment is needed, volunteer service in the school, detention, or even suspension can be arranged. As Dr. Robert E. Fathman, President of the National Coalition to Abolish Corporal Punishment in Schools said, "Good school discipline should be instilled through the mind, not the behind."

(375 words)

Notes punishment：罰　behave：ふるまう、行儀よくする　assume：(当然のことと) 思っている、決めこんでいる　harm：[動] 傷つける、[名] 危害　paddle：平手打ちする　disciplinary：しつけの、懲戒上の　federal：連邦政府の　statistics：統計（調査）　be responsible for ~：~に責任がある　lie：うそをつく　further：さらなる、さらに　violence：暴力　turn into ~：~になる、変わる　loved one：最愛の人　severely：厳しく、激しく　misbehavior：無作法（な振る舞い）　prevent：防ぐ、妨げる　respectful：礼儀正しい、(人に) 敬意を表する　detention：(放課後の) 居残り　suspension：停学　arrange：~を整える、準備する　the National Coalition to Abolish Corporal Punishment in Schools：全米体罰禁止連合　instill：徐々に教え込む

Comprehension Check

1 It can be inferred that the writer of this essay ...
   a. believes that corporal punishment should be used in some schools.
   b. disagrees with the use of hitting as a disciplinary method in school.
   c. believes that parents should discipline their children at home.
   d. is against using punishment in American schools.

2 The writer probably mentions the fact that over 300,000 schoolchildren were disciplined with corporal punishment to show that ...
   a. it is still widely used as a form of punishment in schools in the USA.
   b. Students in the USA do not take school seriously and are irresponsible.
   c. most students misbehave in schools in America.
   d. teachers have no control over students in their classrooms.

3 The word "corporal" in the passage is closest in meaning to:
   a. dangerous   b. harmful   c. painful   d. physical

4 In paragraph 4, the word "they" refers to:
   a. children and parents   b. children
   c. parents   d. teachers and students

5 Choose three sentences that can be used to create a summary of the text.

Corporal punishment is a disciplinary method used in some schools in the USA ...

   a. Corporal punishment may involve hitting, spanking, or paddling students.
   b. Robert Fathman is the director of a national organization against corporal punishment.
   c. Those who support it believe that it helps teach respect and good manners to students.
   d. Teachers should work with parents when deciding whether to use corporal punishment.
   e. Students who are punished never become violent adults.
   f. Those who oppose it do so because of the physical and emotional effects it may have on students.

More Word Chunks

1 Complete the story below, using these word chunks from Unit 10, 11 and 12.

| a couple of | deal with their differences | driving back home | felt guilty | know what to do |
| needed a ride | put his arm around | took a photo | walked away | |

Alyssa and John dated and got along with each other. They accepted each other's personality

and managed to **a.**_____. But their relationship didn't last long.

b._____ weeks ago, when John was **c.**_____

from school, he found one of his classmates, Jessica, walking by the side of the road. He asked her if she **d.**_____, and she accepted his offer. In the car, they talked a lot and had a good time. When they arrived at Jessica's house, she said she wanted her snapshot with John. John **e.**_____ to Alyssa, but he **f.**_____ Jessica and **g.**_____. The next day, when John was with Alyssa, Jessica ran toward him to give him the photo they took. Alyssa got angry and **h.**_____. John didn't **i.**_____.

Notes accept：受け入れる   managed to ...：うまく…する

2 In Units 10 and 12 we learned about the word chunks "take a look" and "take a photo."

The young woman asked the old lady to take a look outside the car.
He told me to take a photo of them together.

Here are some other common word chunks with "take."

take a peek   take a break   take a vacation   take a taxi   take a walk

In Unit 11 we learned about word chunks with "get."

get along with   get my way   get into trouble   get older

Here are some other common chunks with "get."

get around   get back (to)   get away   get together   get out
get up   get by   get over

Change the bold words in the sentence using a word chunk from this page.

a. I've been studying for my English test for two hours and I need to **stop for a while**.

_____

b. I usually take public transportation when I need to **go somewhere** in the city.

_____

c. I find it easy to **meet and talk with** everybody, no matter how old or young.

_____

OUTPUT! Speaking

Make a group, and discuss the following questions.
1. Have you ever been at a school where corporal punishment was used?
2. Do you agree that the use of corporal punishment should be stopped? Why or why not?
3. Are there any cases where teachers are justified in hitting children?
4. What other alternative punishments can you think of?
5. Can you think of any actual cases where corporal punishment has had a bad effect on someone you know?

Notes be justified in：〜が正当化される   alternative：代わりになる、別の

Vocabulary Index

> **Index Notes**
>
> V: verb T: transitive I: intransitive RECIP: reciprocal
> N: noun COUNT: countable UNCOUNT: uncountable VAR: variable SING: singular COLL: collective
> ADJ: adjective ADV: adverb

Word	Definition	Page
accelerate	V-I When a moving vehicle accelerates, it goes faster and faster.	87
act	V-I If someone acts in a particular way, they behave in that way.	25, 26, 62
argue	V-T If you argue that something is true, you state it and give the reasons why you think it is true.	36, 80, 81
attention	N-UNCOUNT Attention is great interest that is shown in someone or something.	52, 53, 73
attitude	N-VAR Your attitude to something is the way that you think and feel about it, especially when this shows in the way you behave.	69
awake	ADJ Someone who is awake is not sleeping.	65
award	N-COUNT An award is a prize or certificate that a person is given for doing something well.	69
beat	V-T If you beat someone or something, you hit them very hard.	90, 91
beg	V-T/ V-I If you beg someone to do something, you ask them very anxiously or eagerly to do it.	37, 57, 79
boarding school	N-VAR A boarding school is a school that some or all of the students live in during the school term.	43
catch up with	PHRASAL VERB If you catch up with someone who is in front of you, you reach them by walking faster than they are walking.	87
celebrity	N-COUNT A celebrity is someone who is famous, especially in areas of entertainment such as movies, music, writing, or sports.	25, 27
challenge	V-T If you challenge someone, you invite them to fight or compete with you in some way.	79
colleague	N-COUNT Your colleagues are the people you work with, especially in a professional job.	78, 87, 89
common	ADJ If something is common, it is found in large numbers or it happens often.	9, 26, 46, 48, 73, 81, 93
community	N-SING-COLL The community is all the people who live in a particular area or place.	91

94 • Vocabulary Index

Word	Definition	Page
company	**N-UNCOUNT** Company is having another person or other people with you, usually when this is pleasant or stops you feeling lonely.	27, 53
compare	**V-T** When you compare things, you consider them and discover the differences or similarities between them.	52, 68
compete	**V-RECIP** If you compete with someone for something, you try to get it for yourself and stop the other person from getting it.	69
computer programmer	**N-COUNT** A computer programmer is a person whose job involves writing programs for computers.	31
conference	**N-COUNT** A conference is a meeting, often lasting a few days, which is organized on a particular subject or to bring together people who have a common interest.	86, 87
confidence	**N-UNCOUNT** If you have confidence, you feel sure about your abilities, qualities, or ideas.	21
confident	**ADJ** If a person or their manner is confident, they feel sure about their own abilities, qualities, or ideas.	20, 21
courage	**N-COUNT** Courage is the quality shown by someone who decides to do something difficult or dangerous, even though they may be afraid.	69
crowd	**N-COUNT-COLL** A crowd is a large group of people who have gathered together, for example, to watch or listen to something interesting, or to protest against something.	43, 88
date	**V-RECIP** If you are dating someone, you go out with them regularly because you are having, or may soon have, a romantic relationship with them. You can also say that two people are dating.	8, 25, 50, 52, 53, 80, 81, 92
dedicate	**V-T** If someone dedicates something such as a book, play, or piece of music to you, they mention your name, for example, in the front of a book or when a piece of music is performed, as a way of showing affection or respect for you.	52, 53
deed	**N-COUNT** A deed is something that is done, especially something that is very good or very bad.	65
determined	**ADJ** If you are determined to do something, you have made a firm decision to do it and will not let anything stop you.	43, 69
diamond	**N-VAR** A diamond is a hard, bright, precious stone that is clear and colorless. Diamonds are used in jewelry and for cutting very hard substances.	65, 82
direct	**ADV** You use direct to describe someone or something reaches their destination without stopping or changing direction, or without involving other people.	15
disagreement	**N-VAR** When there is disagreement about something, people disagree or argue about what should be done.	81
donate	**V-T** If you donate something to a charity or other organization, you give it to them.	56
dormitory	**N-COUNT** A dormitory is a building at a college or university where students live.	21

Word	Definition	Page
encourage	V-T If you encourage someone to do something, you try to persuade them to do it, for example, by telling them that it would be a pleasant thing to do, or by trying to make it easier for them to do it. You can also encourage an activity.	90, 91
environment	N-SING The environment is the natural world of land, sea, air, plants, and animals.	91
eventually	ADV Eventually means at the end of a situation or process or as the final result of it.	15, 32, 53, etc.
expert	N-COUNT An expert is a person who is very skilled at doing something or who knows a lot about a particular subject.	81
factory	N-COUNT A factory is a large building where machines are used to make large quantities of goods.	15
feed	V-I When an animal feeds, it eats or drinks something.	69
fiancé	N-COUNT A woman's fiancé is the man to whom she is engaged to be married.	36, 37, 71
fire	V-T If an employer fires you, they dismiss you from your job.	48
flu	N-UNCOUNT Flu is an illness which is similar to a bad cold but more serious. It often makes you feel very weak and makes your muscles hurt.	21, 35
freshman	N-COUNT In America, a freshman is a student who is in his or her first year at university or college.	59
glad	ADJ If you are glad about something, you are happy and pleased about it.	25, 53, 54
glance	V-I If you glance at something or someone, you look at them very quickly and then look away again immediately.	53
grab	V-T If you grab something, you take it or pick it up suddenly and roughly.	69
grade	N-COUNT Your grade in an examination or piece of written work is the mark you get, usually in the form of a letter or number, that indicates your level of achievement.	35, 49, 59, 71
graduation	N-COUNT A graduation is a special ceremony at a university, college, or school, at which degrees and diplomas are given to students who have successfully completed their studies.	43, 59
grateful	ADJ If you are grateful for something that someone has given you or done for you, you have warm, friendly feelings toward them and wish to thank them.	59
greet	V-T When you greet someone, you say 'Hello' or shake hands with them.	15
guard	N-COUNT A guard is someone such as a soldier, police officer, or prison officer who is guarding a particular place or person.	71, 78
guess	V-T/V-I You say "I guess" to show that you are slightly uncertain or reluctant about what you are saying.	6, 8, 9, 24, etc.

Word	Definition	Page
guy	N-COUNT A guy is a man.	53
hairy	ADJ Someone or something that is hairy is covered with hair.	74, 75
happen	V-T If you happen to do something, you do it by chance. If it happens that something is the case, it occurs by chance.	29, 40, 46, 53, etc.
heartbroken	ADJ Someone who is heartbroken is very sad and emotionally upset.	37
hitchhiker	N-COUNT A hitchhiker is someone who travels by getting lifts from passing vehicles without paying.	74, 75
hop	V-I When birds and some small animals hop, they move along by jumping on both feet.	87, 89
independent	ADJ If someone is independent, they do not need help or money from anyone else.	9, 36
inspire	V-T If something or someone inspires a particular book, work of art, or action, they are the source of the ideas in it or act as a model for it.	68, 69, 70
instant	N-SING If you say that something happens at a particular instant, you mean that it happens at exactly the time you have been referring to, and you are usually suggesting that it happens quickly or immediately.	12, 47, 53
internship	N-COUNT An internship is the position held by an advanced student or a recent graduate, especially in medicine, who is being given practical training under supervision.	30, 31
kid	N-COUNT You can refer to a child as a kid.	58, 59, 60, 88
lack	V-T/V-I If you say that someone or something lacks a particular quality or that a particular quality is lacking in them, you mean that they do not have any or enough of it.	21
laughter	N-UNCOUNT Laughter is the sound of people laughing, for example, because they are amused or happy.	21
local	ADJ Local means existing in or belonging to the area where you live, or to the area that you are talking about.	15, 27, 51
locker	N-COUNT A locker is a small metal or wooden cabinet with a lock, where you can put your personal possessions, for example in a school, place of work, or sports club.	59
lonely	ADJ Someone who is lonely is unhappy because they are alone or do not have anyone they can talk to.	37, 38, 51
madly	ADV You can use madly to indicate that one person loves another a great deal.	81, 82
Native-American	N-COUNT Native Americans are people from any of the many groups who were already living in North America before Europeans arrived.	43
nerd	N-COUNT If you say that someone is a nerd, you mean that they are unpopular or boring, especially because they wear unfashionable clothes or show too much interest in computers or science. [INFORMAL]	58, 59

Word	Definition	Page
nightclub	N-COUNT A nightclub is a place where people go late in the evening to drink and dance.	25, 52, 53
opposite	N-COUNT The opposite of someone or something is the person or thing that is most different from them.	21
part-time	ADJ If someone is a part-time worker or has a part-time job, they work for only part of each day or week.	30, 31
passenger	N-COUNT A passenger in a vehicle such as a bus, boat, or plane is a person who is traveling in it, but who is not driving it or working on it.	75
pick up	PHRASAL VERB When you pick up someone or something that is waiting to be collected, you go to the place where they are and take them away, often in a car.	56, 59, 60, 75
psychologist	N-COUNT A psychologist is a person who studies the human mind and tries to explain why people behave in the way that they do.	9, 27
qualification	N-COUNT Your qualifications are the official documents or titles you have that show your level of education and training.	30, 31
rare	ADJ Something that is rare is not common and is therefore interesting or valuable.	9
recipe	N-SING If you say that something is a recipe for a particular situation, you mean that it is likely to result in that situation.	81
reconsider	V-T/V-I If you reconsider a decision or opinion, you think about it and try to decide whether it should be changed.	81
remind	V-T If you say that someone or something reminds you of another person or thing, you mean that they are similar to the other person or thing and that they make you think about them.	53
resent	V-T If you resent someone or something, you feel bitter and angry about them.	81
reservation	N-COUNT A reservation is an area of land that is kept separate for a particular group of people to live in.	43
respect	V-T If you respect someone's wishes, rights, or customs, you avoid doing things that they would dislike or regard as wrong.	51, 80, 81
responsibility	N-COUNT If you have responsibility for something or someone, or if they are your responsibility, it is your job or duty to deal with them and to make decisions relating to them.	91
retire	V-I When older people retire, they leave their job and usually stop working completely.	14, 15
reward	N-COUNT A reward is a sum of money offered to anyone who can give information about lost or stolen property, a missing person, or someone who is wanted by the police.	40
risk	V-T If you risk doing something, you do it, even though you know that it might have undesirable consequences.	63, 65

Word	Definition	Page
roll	V-I If you roll somewhere, you move on a surface while lying down, turning your body over and over, so that you are sometimes on your back, sometimes on your side, and sometimes on your front.	65
romantic	ADJ Something that is romantic is beautiful in a way that strongly affects your feelings.	80
salary	N-VAR A salary is the money that someone earns each month or year from their employer.	30, 31
scholarship	N-COUNT If you get a scholarship to a school or university, your studies are paid for by the school or university or by some other organization.	43
security	N-COUNT A feeling of security is a feeling of being safe and free from worry.	31, 78
shore	N-COUNT The shores or the shore of a sea, lake, or wide river is the land along the edge of it.	69, 71
spot	V-T If you spot something or someone, you notice them.	87
stranger	N-COUNT A stranger is someone you have never met before.	9, 74
talkative	ADJ Someone who is talkative talks a lot.	9, 20, 36
taste	N-UNCOUNT A person's taste is their choice in the things that they like or buy, for example, their clothes, possessions, or music.	8, 9, 29
tattoo	N-COUNT A tattoo is a design that is drawn on someone's skin using needles to make little holes and filling them with colored dye.	74, 75
tend	V-T If something tends to happen, it usually happens or it often happens.	9, 12, 13, 32, 46
tough	ADJ A tough person is strong and determined, and can tolerate difficulty or suffering.	21, 36, 37, 59
treat	V-T If you treat someone or something in a particular way, you behave toward them or deal with them in that way.	7
upset	ADJ If you are upset, you are unhappy or disappointed because something bad has happened to you.	37, 48, 52, 53
valuable	ADJ Valuable objects are objects that are worth a lot of money.	65
volunteer	N-COUNT A volunteer is someone who offers to do a particular task or job without being forced to do it.	9, 49, 91
wrinkle	N-COUNT Wrinkles are lines that form on someone's face as they grow old.	75
yell	V-T/V-I If you yell, you shout loudly, usually because you are excited, angry, or in pain.	21, 81

JPCA 本書は日本出版著作権協会（JPCA）が委託管理する著作物です。
複写（コピー）・複製、その他著作物の利用については、事前に JPCA（電
話 03-3812-9424、e-mail:info@e-jpca.com）の許諾を得て下さい。なお、
日本出版著作権協会 無断でコピー・スキャン・デジタル化等の複製をすることは著作権法上
http://www.e-jpca.com/ の例外を除き、著作権法違反となります。

A Good Read 1　Developing Strategies for Effective Reading Student Book
1st Edition
Carlos Islam
Carrie Steenburgh
Copyright © 2009 by Cengage Learning Asia Pte Ltd
ALL RIGHTS RESERVED.
No part of this work covered by the copyright hereon may be reproduced, transmitted, stored,
or used in any form or by any means – graphic, electronic, or mechanical, including but not limited
to photocopying, recording, scanning, digitizing, taping, Web distribution, information networks,
or information storage and retrieval systems – without the prior written permission of the publisher.

A Good Read 1　Developing Strategies for Effective Reading
Pre-Intermediate　▶▶Japan Edition

2017 年 4 月 10 日　初版第 1 刷発行
2024 年 4 月 15 日　初版第 4 刷発行

著　者　Carlos Islam ／ Carrie Steenburgh
監修者　竹内 理
編著者　佐々木顕彦

発行者　森　信久
発行所　株式会社　松 柏 社
　　　　〒 102-0072　東京都千代田区飯田橋 1-6-1
　　　　TEL　03 (3230) 4813（代表）
　　　　FAX　03 (3230) 4857
　　　　http://www.shohakusha.com
　　　　e-mail: info@shohakusha.com

装丁　　　　　　　小島トシノブ（NONdesign）
挿絵　　　　　　　うえむらのぶこ
本文レイアウト組版　高橋里沙

印刷・製本　シナノ書籍印刷株式会社

略号＝ 719

Copyright © 2017 by Osamu Takeuchi, Akihiko Sasaki
本書を無断で複写・複製することを禁じます。